UPPER INTERMEDIATE

Language
LEADER
WORKBOOK
and Audio CD

T0346011

Grant Kempton

CONTENTS

LANGUAGE LEADER   UPPER INTERMEDIATE

CONTENTS

Communication

1.1 GREAT COMMUNICATORS?

1 Fill the gaps with one word. The first two letters are given to help you.

1 It's not enough to speak well. You have to have a good ap_pearance_ too.

2 His grammar is good but he doesn't have an extensive vo_____.

3 He has a terrible sense of hu_____. His jokes are terrible!

4 He's a ra_____. He can never talk about one topic.

5 He's boring to listen to because he speaks at a slow pa_____.

6 I could tell you about how I planned the project but I don't want to di_____.

7 I don't trust him. He never makes eye co_____.

8 Everybody loves John. He has so much ch_____!

9 Don't only listen to the words. Read the body la_____.

10 I never pass exams because I suffer from ne_____.

11 It's important to know that there are differences between cu_____, especially between the Japanese and the Americans.

12 He's a wonderful li_____ – he never interrupts and is very sympathetic.

2a Match the words with the correct meaning.

| endeavour devotion sweltering injustice |
| oppression transform unceasingly fulfil |
| harmony despair discord ~~shrink from~~ |

1 verb – to avoid doing something difficult or unpleasant
shrink from

2 noun – when people are treated in a cruel or unfair way _____, _____

3 noun – when you love someone a lot and show this by giving them attention _____

4 verb – to do or achieve something that you have promised to do or should do _____

5 noun – when people are not arguing, fighting or disagreeing _____

6 noun – a feeling that you have no hope at all _____

7 adjective – very very hot _____

8 noun – an attempt to try to do something new or difficult _____

9 verb – to change someone or something completely _____

10 adverb – without stopping _____

11 noun – disagreement between people _____

2b Complete the text with words from above.

Today the weather is ¹_____ but not too hot that I will ²_____ from my endeavour. 'What is it?' you ask. I will tell you. I will ³_____ discord into harmony. There will be no place for ⁴_____, oppression or despair. As our good friend said 'Love each other every day ⁵_____ and then we will learn to love ourselves!'

2c Find examples of the following in the text above.

a) repetition   c) contrast

b) tripling   d) a quote

3 1.2 Listen and write the number of syllables in each word. Then underline the stressed syllable.

1 en_dea_vour _3_   7 devotion

2 sweltering   8 injustice

3 oppression   9 transform

4 unceasingly   10 harmony

5 despair   11 discord

6 shrink   12 fulfil

1 Match sentences 1–7 with the words describing simple and continuous aspect a–g.

1 I have blue eyes. _d)_

2 He was preparing the documents for you last night but he didn't finish. ___

3 Right now I'm looking for a new house. ___

4 Steven goes to the gym three times a week. ___

5 I'm staying at my brother's until I find a new flat. ___

6 I sent the email at six o'clock. ___

7 More people are studying courses in media today than ever before. ___

a) temporary

b) habitual

c) complete

d) permanent

e) unfinished

f) in progress

g) changing

2 Complete the text with the right aspect for each verb: simple or continuous in the present or past tense.

Today diplomats [1] _are attempting_ (attempt) to avoid a major political disaster. Yesterday, UN representative, Petr Hulavac [2]_____ (give) a speech on European-Asian relations. In his speech he [3]_____ (say) 'Although some countries [4]_____ (try) to make life difficult for us, we [5]_____ (still work) to create a better environment for economic cooperation.'

Unfortunately, the simultaneous translation to Asian delegates [6]_____ (be): 'Although Asian countries [7]_____ (make) life impossible for us …'. Mr Hulavac [8]_____ (have) breakfast this morning when angry Chinese officials [9]_____ (interrupt) his meal to make a formal complaint. Mr Hulavac was understandably very angry. 'This type of mistake [10]_____ (not be) acceptable in the UN and we are now investigating how this could happen.' Last night, security [11]_____ (look for) the translators involved, but they have mysteriously disappeared. This morning the Head of Security [12]_____ (suggest) that this may be an attempt by an outside organisation to upset work at the UN.

LISTENING

3 1.3 Listen to a talk about subtitling. Put the things that the speaker mentions in the right order.

a) What are subtitles? _1_

b) Why comedy is difficult to translate. ___

c) Why people can easily find mistakes. ___

d) Subtitling and dubbing ___

e) An example of bad translation ___

4 1.3 Listen again and answer the questions.

1 Where can you find the subtitles in a film?

_____

2 What kind of people easily find mistakes in subtitles?

_____

3 What did one actor want to say about his friend?

_____

4 Why do people sometimes laugh at the wrong time in a subtitled film?

_____

5 How many advantages does the speaker give for dubbing?

_____

6 Which language dubbing does the speaker talk about in his example?

_____

Where computers can't go ... *translation*

One of the great dreams that people had about computers was that they would break down the language barriers between people. It was thought that computers would be able to translate articles from one language to another and even, once voice recognition was in place, translate what we say. 1____

2____ Most people in the nineties believed that by 2007 all computers would be able to translate from one international website to another. However, this does not seem to have happened. Here is an example of an Internet translation (from German) of information about a footballer. 'In season 2006/07 played he in the Upper League team in the team and has a total of seven minutes active no further add, as he number among professionals only 4th goalkeeper. His 2007 expiring contract was signed by the team not renewed.' While this translation gave me the information I needed, it is certainly not a good translation.

3____ However the results are very similar. Even the most popular CAT programme, Babelfish, although better than the translation above, was still far from perfect.

4____ One reason for this is that computer programmers are not language specialists. In the world of mathematics, for example, with algebra you just replace one symbol with another. Unfortunately translation does not work like this. Translators have to think about the situation and what the writer is trying to say. There are no idioms in mathematics, for example. In short, translation is not a simple task and there is no 'key'.

5____ Translation, as any professional translator will tell you, is not like mathematics and while computer programmers are still working alone in their little room with their mathematical ideas, translation programmes won't get any better.

READ BETTER

In each paragraph of a text there is usually one sentence that gives you the general meaning of that paragraph. There are three kinds of sentence:

1 The Thesis Statement   This will give you the overall topic of the text and is usually found at the end of the introductory paragraph.

2 The Topic Sentence   This sentence will give you the topic of the paragraph. It is usually the first sentence of the paragraph but not always.

3 The Concluding Sentence   This sentence will summarise the whole text and is usually found at the beginning of the conclusion.

5 Read the text about computer translation. Match sentences A–E with gaps 1–5. Think about whether the sentences are a thesis statement, topic sentence or concluding sentence.

A Computer Assisted Translation (CAT) was the biggest hope for automatic translation on computers.

B In conclusion, it seems to be that most people now agree that the dream will stay a dream.

C This article will look at what has happened over the last few years and show that the dream still hasn't come true.

D There seems to be a number of reasons why CAT has not provided good translations.

E There are many types of CAT programmes, other than the one I used in the above example.

VOCABULARY: idioms

6 Write an idiom to describe each situation.

1 He could have told her he liked the present. Instead he told her it was the wrong colour.

think before you speak
_____

2 It's amazing. I bought him the new book by David Steel and he bought the same book for me!

_____

3 Simon told Jane and Peter told me.

_____

4 He sounds polite, but look at the way he eats. Disgusting!

_____

READING

1 Read the article. In which paragraph does the writer talk about …

1 teenagers not listening to parents. ____

2 examples of things parents shouldn't say. ____

3 what listening parents do. ____

4 a different language that teenagers speak. ____

5 whether parents talk with or at their children. ____

2 Read the text again and decide if these statements are true or false.

1 Parents who talk at teenagers fail to communicate effectively. ____

2 Parents often don't understand what teenagers are saying. ____

3 Parents wish teenagers would listen more and talk less. ____

4 Parents should listen without emotion. ____

5 There is nothing wrong with what parents say to teenagers. ____

Do parents and teenagers really talk?

A 'My parents don't listen to me!' This is the most common complaint teenagers have about their parents. Even teens who generally get along well with their parents wish they would listen more, talk with them more, be less critical and judgmental, and be more willing to discuss the teen's point of view.

B Parents, on the other hand, have the same complaint: 'He won't listen to me!' Parents complain that teens are silent, or moody, aggressive and loud. They wish their teens would share more and talk with them in a friendly fashion. They wish their teens would listen more and criticise them less.

C Unfortunately, the style of much parent/teen communication is negative and ineffective. Parents should ask themselves, 'Do I talk **at** my teenager or do I talk **with** my teenager?' Parents who talk **at** teens are often reminding, threatening, blaming, questioning, ordering or judging. This style is used to pressure teens into doing something parents want them to do, and the effect is decreased effective communication.

D How would adults feel about these comments: 'That dress is too tight!' 'The lawn looks terrible. Are you even too lazy to cut the grass right?' 'Why can't you be more like Sam?' 'Eat your salad!' Would they remain friends with a person who made such remarks to them? Can they hear echoes of their own voice talking **at** their teen?

E Parents who talk **with** teenagers listen. They listen to what teens are thinking, feeling or wanting to do. They try to understand and accept teens' points of view. In addition, they are not afraid to express their own views or share feelings and concerns.

F The relationship between parents and teens is often highly emotional. Their relationship is changing, and both parents and teens want to be heard, understood and accepted. If this is to be achieved, parents especially must listen with their hearts as well as their heads.

G What is becoming more and more common, however, in the Age of the Internet, is that teenagers are beginning to speak a new language – a language that parents do not understand. 'Teenspeak' is a product of instant messaging and Internet chat, worlds teenagers spend an increasing amount of time in. Teenspeak has also become popular through modern music. The fact that teenagers are not understood by their parents and parents cannot understand what their children are saying is yet another reason why communication breaks down. Seems like parents need to go back to school …

GRAMMAR:
the perfect aspect

3 Correct the sentences, making *one* correction in form.

1 He ~~has~~ went to France six times between 1978 and 2002.

2 Had you meet the Chancellor last week?

3 He couldn't graduate because he hasn't passed the course.

4 Has he forgot the plans again?

5 The new injections had not stop the spread of the disease. We need to find another cure.

6 Had the bank took a loan before they declared themselves bankrupt?

7 I have give the samples to the laboratory and we are now waiting for the results.

8 He has had the car for three years until he sold it last month.

4 Complete the letter with the word in brackets in the correct form: past simple, present perfect or past perfect.

Dear Jenny,
Please help me. I have two children, Sarah who is five and is an angel and Lawrence who is a teenager and driving me crazy. For example, last week he ¹_____ (leave) the house and ²_____ (not come) back for three days. Before last week he ³_____ (never do) this. I ⁴_____ (try) everything the books tell you to do. Over the last few months, I ⁵_____ (be) understanding and polite to him but every time I ⁶_____ (speak) to him he ⁷_____ (get) angry and ⁸_____ (start) to shout at me. Until last year he ⁹_____ (be) a good boy and ¹⁰_____ (always help) me at home. What can I do?

LISTENING

5 **1.4** Listen to a radio show about language and choose the correct answer a, b or c.

1 What is Ola's favourite drink?
a) kebab   b) latte   c) bruschetta

2 A 'screenager' is
a) a lazy boy   b) a kind of computer
c) a teenager who uses a computer a lot

3 When do you have 'brunch'?
a) mid-morning   b) early morning
c) lunchtime

A Bollywood production

4 What does the 'B' in 'Bollywood' stand for?
a) Bengal   b) big   c) Bombay

5 What are the two words in 'motel'
a) mini hotel   b) motor hotel   c) mobile hotel

6 What are TLAs?
a) initial letters as words   b) very long words
c) words people don't say

6 Give three examples of TLAs.

1 _____

2 _____

3 _____

LEARN BETTER

Using a dictionary can sometimes cause problems, not solve them. Consider these suggestions:

1 Use a monolingual dictionary, not a bilingual dictionary. Bilingual dictionaries are not written for language students and often don't have all the meanings or enough example sentences.

2 Choose a dictionary at your level of English. This means that the meanings of the words are easy to understand, as are the example sentences.

3 Don't choose the first meaning. Often it will be the wrong one. Words have many meanings, so make sure you check all the meanings.

4 Check the example sentences before choosing the right meaning.

5 If you're looking for an idiom or phrase, don't only look for the first word. Maybe another word is more important.

DICTATION

1 [1.5] Listen and write what you hear.

_____

_____

_____

_____

_____

_____

_____

_____

KEY LANGUAGE:
outlining problems, offering solutions

2 Complete each sentence with two words.

1 I think the best way to _____ _____ this is for the club to pay for Claudio's brother …

2 _____ _____ is that Claudio doesn't speak any English …

3 I think that seems to be _____ _____ forward but we'd better talk to Claudio and the club quickly.

4 Yes, I can see it's _____ _____ difficult situation.

5 It's a very _____ _____, isn't it?

6 That might _____ _____ the problem, but what will his brother do in England?

7 The _____ _____ that is that if his brother is out working, Claudio won't see him …

8 I'm sure we can _____ _____ out, but we don't have much time to do it.

9 As you can see, it's _____ _____ circle for both Claudio and the club.

3a Put the sentences in Exercise 2 in the right gap in the conversation.

A: All right. So, we need to get the contract signed by the end of the day. I'm sure Claudio wants to sign and the club certainly wants him. a _8_

B: b____ and he's not sure he can come and live in England alone.

A: c____ Would language classes help?

B: Well, there's the problem. If Claudio attends intensive English classes, which he needs, he won't be able to train properly and without proper training he won't play well. If he doesn't play well, then the club loses. On the other hand, if he can't speak English, he'll be unhappy and won't play well and again the club loses. d____

A: Hmm. e____ Does Claudio have a family?

B: Yes. He is very close to his brother, who speaks good English.

A: Good. f____ to come with him to England and live with him for the first year.

B: g____ He has a job back home.

A: The club could find him one, couldn't they?

B: h____ during the day, when he will need his brother's help the most.

A: OK, then the club will pay him to be his brother's helper. It'll cost them more money but if Claudio is such a good player, they'll think it's worth it. What do you think?

B: Yes. i____

3b [1.6] Listen to the conversation and check your answers.

STUDY SKILLS: note-taking

1 [1.7] Listen to part of a short talk about teaching children to speak. Write the phrases that the speaker uses to signpost the following sections.

1 Introducing what is to come

_____

2 Sequencing

_____

3 Signalling the main point

_____

4 Rephrasing

_____

5 Exemplifying

_____

2 [1.7] There are four mistakes in the notes below. Listen again and correct them.

Topic – Why C should learn
2 langs

Main points
1 How C learn 2 langs
2 Disadvs of lrning 2 langs
3 Advs of lrning 2 langs

1 – Most Important Thing
– Learn at S and H diff,
e.g. H read and write
Mum says 'mama' 'dada' for 3
or 4 mnths before baby says it

WRITING SKILLS: formal and informal emails

3 Tick the phrases below that are informal.

Dear Mr Jones

Once again, I would like to apologise …

Yours sincerely

Thank you for your email asking me to …

If you wish, I could …

Thanks for sending me …

See attached

Great meeting last week!

Hope to hear from you soon

I look forward to hearing from you

Sorry, but I can't …

4 Your colleague has written an email to a customer (Mr Jones) but your boss thinks it is too informal. He has asked you to rewrite it in a formal style. Read the informal email and then rewrite it formally, making sure you use all the relevant information and using some of the phrases from Exercise 3.

Hi Paul!
Thanks for your email yesterday. I'm sorry but I won't be able to come this week.
If you want, I can ask someone else to come. Let me know what you think. In the meantime, any problems or queries please let me know.
Best Paul.

_____

_____

_____

_____

_____

_____

_____

Environment

2.1 URBAN ENVIRONMENT

VOCABULARY: local environment

1 Complete the sentences with the correct word combinations.

traffic congestion	mindless vandalism
rush hour	transport connections
detached house	noise pollution
stunning views	~~abandoned cars~~
apartment block	crime rate

1 The park is full of _abandoned cars._ People just drive up and leave them there.

2 The _____ in my area aren't very good – it often takes me a long time to get anywhere.

3 I live on the 25th floor of an _____.

4 I live in a _____ with a big garden round it.

5 Why destroy the bus stop? That's just _____!

6 Do not drive through the centre of town at 5.30 p.m. It's the _____ then.

7 On Friday nights the open-air disco plays music very loud until 3 a.m. I think that's _____!

8 Lorries are not allowed into the city centre because of _____.

9 The rise in the _____ in the last few months is shocking. The police should do something.

10 Have a look from the balcony. There are _____ from there.

PRONUNCIATION

2 1.8 Listen and write the number of syllables in each word combination.

1 cosmopolitan atmosphere _5 – 3_

2 open spaces _____

3 abandoned cars _____

4 transport connections _____

5 mindless vandalism _____

6 stunning views _____

VOCABULARY: words from the lesson

3 Fill the gaps in the text with one word. The first two letters are given to help you.

A [1] st<u>udy</u> was carried out last week, [2] de_____ to measure how many people like nuts in their chocolate. The [3] fi_____ were very surprising. Chocolate without nuts [4] ra_____ much more highly than chocolate with nuts. The survey also [5] es_____ that more than 30 percent of people who responded had, or knew someone who had, an allergy to nuts. Nut allergy seems to be becoming a big [6] is_____ and this research, [7] ca_____ out for chocolate manufacturers, agrees with scientists who say that our immunity to allergies is weakening. This may, of course, explain why chocolate without nuts was more popular than chocolate with nuts.

TRANSLATION

4 Translate these word combinations into your language. Do they exist in your language? If not, what do you say instead?

1 mindless vandalism _____

2 detached house _____

3 transport connections _____

4 rush hour _____

5 traffic congestion _____

6 crime rate _____

7 noise pollution _____

8 stunning views _____

GRAMMAR: present perfect simple and continuous

1a Match sentence halves 1–6 with a–f.

1 They have finished ___

2 The zoo has been feeding ___

3 The species has become ___

4 No one has fed ___

5 The government has been reducing ___

6 I have turned down ___

a) extinct because of too much hunting.

b) CO_2 emissions since 2006.

c) the tests and are now waiting for the results.

d) the temperature because it was too hot.

e) three lion cubs since they were born.

f) the polar bears today.

1b Have the activities/situations above finished or are they ongoing? Tick the correct box.

	Have finished / taken place	Ongoing or continuing
1	☐	☐
2	☐	☐
3	☐	☐
4	☐	☐
5	☐	☐
6	☐	☐

2 Complete the sentences with the verb in brackets in the correct form (present perfect simple or continuous).

A According to the article, we _____ (look) at the wrong issue since 1975.

B For the past three years, many scientists _____ (say) something completely different.

C At some time, I'm sure we _____ (all think) about hotter temperatures, rising water levels and the possible effects for people around the world.

D Some scientists _____ (make) the same point – that the 'cycle' theory shows us that we can be sure the world is going to get cold again soon.

E Because of global warming, in recent years icebergs _____ (shrink) and there _____ (be) more and more rain.

F Secondly, the increase in heat is not because of natural increases in temperature, but because we _____ (damage) the environment.

G Since then, we _____ (live) through the beginning of a cold period.

READING

READ BETTER

Most sentences in a text refer back to what was written before or to what will be written next. Look at number 1 in Exercise 3, which has been done for you. 'Hotter temperatures, rising water levels' in sentence C are examples of global warming, which is mentioned in the sentence before. Also, in sentence C we have the words *we* and *all*. In the sentence before we can see *we have all been hearing*. When you do this exercise, look at the sentence before and after the gap to help you and you will learn how sentences in a text link to each other.

3 Read the article on climate change. Match sentences A–G in Exercise 2 with gaps 1–7.

4 Read the article again and answer the questions.

1 What two examples of global warming are given in the first paragraph?

_____

2 How many articles did Newsweek write about Global Cooling?

_____

3 What has been happening since 1965?

_____

4 Why is it wrong to wait any longer for evidence?

_____

5 Which groups don't like the global warming theory?

_____

6 Why are ice and rain different from sea water?

_____

5 There are five word combinations in the article from the article on page 18 of the Course book. Underline them.

DICTATION

6 1.9 Listen and write what the man says. Check that the word combinations used are the same as the ones you underlined in Exercise 5.

_____

_____

_____

_____

_____

_____

7 Complete the notes.

1 The article was in a _____.

2 _____ makes people happier.

3 The article gives a _____ of life after climate change.

CLIMATE CHANGE: GLOBAL COOLING, GLOBAL WARMING ... OR SOMETHING ELSE?

IN RECENT YEARS WE HAVE all been hearing about global warming. [1] *C* It seems that the issue has been decided. There is global warming and we can't do anything to stop it.
Well, actually this might not be the whole story. In 1975, Newsweek published an article about Global Cooling, not Global Warming. The theory behind it was this: 'In recent years (1940–1965), global temperatures have been getting colder. World history shows that Hot Periods and Cold Periods appear in cycles. The period up to 1940 was a hot period. [2] ___' This theory was supported by very famous scientists in scientific journals, and also

celebrities, including Isaac Asimov.
Yet, in 2006, Newsweek wrote an 'apology' article. [3] ___ It isn't global *cooling* but global *warming* that is the big issue. There are two reasons for this. Firstly, there was a cooling period between 1940 and 1965. Since then, however temperatures have been increasing. [4] ___
So, do we all agree that global warming is the thing to worry about? Well, surprisingly the answer to that is 'no'. There are still many people who do not accept the theory about 'global warming'. [5] ___ Other scientists argue that there is not enough evidence over a long period

of time. Well, in fact, that's true but if we wait for a longer period, it may be too late to do anything about it!
Finally, of course, large countries with strong economies that use a lot of power, and 'interested' industries (like the oil industry) spend millions and millions of dollars on research, trying to disprove the global warming theory.
They might be right. Maybe we are getting a false impression of what is happening. Why? [6] ___ They say it is going to get much colder. This is the 'Arctic Stream' theory. It is a very complex theory but here is the simple version: The UK is warmer than Canada because it has a

stream of salt water that keeps it hot. This is called the 'Gulf Stream'. As we all know, salt water is warmer than fresh water (is it warmer to swim in the sea or a lake?). [7] ___ Ice and rain are fresh water, not salt water. This will have a significant effect on the Gulf Stream. With more fresh water in the sea, the Gulf Stream will stop working. If it stops working, the UK and Northern Europe will get much, much colder.
So, what should we believe? Climate change is not such a simple issue. If you live in Northern Europe, it looks like you are going to get very cold. For the rest of us, time to get the sun cream out.

GRAMMAR: indirect questions

1 Peter Smith is interviewing Dr Aleyna Aykut about an earthquake in Istanbul. Correct the indirect questions he asks.

1 I'd like know how many earthquakes has Istanbul had.

I'd like to know how many earthquakes Istanbul has had.

2 Could you tell when was the last earthquake in Istanbul?

_____

3 I can ask when the last big earthquake in Turkey was?

_____

4 Could you tell me the Izmit earthquake was close to Istanbul?

_____

5 Do you know how many people in the Izmit earthquake were killed?

_____

6 Do you know whether did the Izmit earthquake affect Istanbul?

_____

7 Could you tell me is there a strong possibility of an earthquake in Istanbul?

_____

LISTENING

2 1.10 Listen to the first part of the interview and check your answers to Exercise 1.

3 1.10 Listen again and answer the questions from Exercise 1.

1 _____
2 _____
3 _____
4 _____
5 _____
6 _____
7 _____

4a 1.11 Some researchers are preparing the questions for the second part of the interview. Listen and finish the questions they decide to use.

1 Why do you think an earthquake _____?
2 How big _____?
3 What will happen if _____?
4 What _____?
5 Is the _____?
6 Are there any _____?
7 Should _____?
8 Can you predict _____?

4b Turn the questions above into indirect questions.

1 Can I ask _____?
2 Do you know _____?
3 Could you tell me _____?
4 I'd like to know _____.
5 Can I ask _____?
6 Do you know _____?
7 Could you tell me _____?
8 I'd like to know _____.

READING

5 Read some of the answers taken from the second part of the interview. Which questions from Exercise 4 do they answer?

Q: _____

A: Absolutely not. There's no point worrying about something that might not happen. We can only say that an earthquake will probably happen, not that it will definitely happen. The government is working hard to make people safe.

Q: _____

A: Unfortunately we do not have the technology to do that. We believe there is a 62 percent chance in the next 30 years, a 50 percent chance in the next 25 years, and over the next ten years about 32 percent that a major earthquake in Istanbul will happen.

Q: _____

A: This is possibly the biggest problem in Istanbul. Some houses are taller than others but they may be connected to the same structure or 'column' as the house next to them. This column may be shorter or taller. This is very bad for the safety of a house. Another problem is that many buildings have shops on the ground floor. This means that there are not enough rooms and so not enough walls to hold the weight of the building.

Q: _____

A: We can't be sure, but it will be similar to the Izmit earthquake, probably a strength of 6.8 to 7.5. Without proper preparation we think this would result in the collapse of over 500,000 buildings and the deaths of thousands of people.

VOCABULARY: adverbs

6 Complete the text with adverbs from the box. One adverb is not used.

> perhaps   pensively   mainly   normally
> deliberately   relatively

Unlike Istanbul, there are ^{1}_____ few earthquakes in Izmit. ^{2}_____, earthquakes happen in summer but they could ^{3}_____ happen at any time. Izmit needs to take steps to protect itself, ^{4}_____ in the area of improving the safety of its buildings. Now, most engineers are ^{5}_____ building earthquake-protected buildings.

EXTRA VOCABULARY: more adverbs

You can usually make adverbs from nouns by adding -ly. Be careful, however – not all adverbs end in -ly. Also not all adverbs have nouns and/or adjectives (e.g. *perhaps*).

7 Complete the table below. Some of the adverbs are in the Course book and others are in Exercise 6. You may want to check their meaning in your dictionary.

Noun	Adjective	Adverb
✗	absolute	
✗	normal	
intention		
✗	fast	
ease		
✗	slow	
completion		
✗	immediate	
probability		

KEY LANGUAGE: agreeing and disagreeing politely, polite questions

1 Correct these sentences.

a) You have point, but you don't think the answer is too simple?

_____

b) I am interested know more about it.

_____

c) I would go long you there.

_____

d) What is very truth because it can only generate small amounts of electricity.

_____

e) You have absolute right!

_____

f) I would know how you discovered that.

_____

g) That's one type to look at it but what else they can choose?

_____

2a Match sentences a–g in Exercise 1 with gaps 1–7.

A: Let's talk about the government decision on alternative sources of power. It seems they won't agree to wave power.

B: ¹___ No one's been told yet!

A: A friend at a newspaper told me. They're going to announce their decision tomorrow. I believe they think it's too expensive.

D: ²___ They think it's too expensive and too slow.

B: What about solar power? It's certainly not as expensive as wave power.

A: ³___ I'm sure they have already thought about solar power.

B: Well, ⁴___ There isn't another choice!

A: What about this new 'sugar power'? I read something in a report and ⁵___ It's certainly something I know very little about.

D: ⁶___ Peter Davis thinks it could be really useful.

B: Oh come on! It's useless!

C: For our purposes ⁷___, I'm afraid.

A: Well then, what are we going to do?

2b 🔊 1.12 Listen to the meeting and check your answers.

VOCABULARY: words from the lesson

3 Complete the sentences with the words in the box.

viable	solar	spoil	fossil	renewable
wave	eyesore	generate		

1 We use this machine to _____ electricity when there is a power cut.

2 Coal is a _____ fuel.

3 We have a _____ panel on our roof to take power from the sun.

4 Making a car powered by water is not a _____ idea. Each car would need huge amounts of water.

5 The landscape would be beautiful if they hadn't built a football stadium there. The stadium is an _____.

6 That little machine with all the water inside is an example of _____ power.

7 Building a power station there will _____ my view of the sea.

8 Although it is more expensive, we will never be without _____ energy.

WRITING SKILLS:
writing a questionnaire

1a Complete the question types with the phrases in the box.

> yes or no   a figure   *what, who, why, etc.*
> how frequently   a number on
> ~~choice between~~   to tick items

1 Questions requiring a *choice between* alternatives.

2 Questions which require the respondent to choose _____ a scale.

3 Closed questions requiring the answer _____.

4 Questions which require a respondent to indicate _____ they do something.

5 Open questions beginning with _____.

6 Straightforward questions which require _____ or a limited number of words.

7 Questions requiring respondents _____ in lists or boxes.

1b Match questions A–G with the types 1–7 above.

A How many children are there in your family?   _6_

B Is this your first car?

   Yes ☐ No ☐   ____

C How often do you visit the library in a week?

   a) Once   b) Twice   c) More than twice
   d) Never   ____

D On a scale of 1–5 (5 being the highest), how much do you like chocolate?   ____

E What is the best meal you have ever eaten?   ____

F Which of the following would you prefer?

   a) a park for kids   b) a new cinema   ____

G Tick which things you own.

   mobile phone ☐   a laptop ☐
   a GPS system ☐   an iPod ☐
   a portable DVD player ☐   ____

2 Write one of each type of question to find out the information asked for in this note.

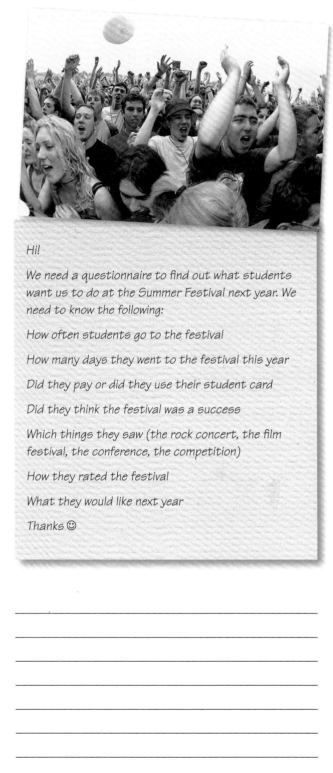

Hi!

We need a questionnaire to find out what students want us to do at the Summer Festival next year. We need to know the following:

How often students go to the festival

How many days they went to the festival this year

Did they pay or did they use their student card

Did they think the festival was a success

Which things they saw (the rock concert, the film festival, the conference, the competition)

How they rated the festival

What they would like next year

Thanks ☺

_____
_____
_____
_____
_____
_____
_____
_____

3 Sport

3.1 THE BEAUTIFUL GAME

1a Complete the words that refer to people in sport.

1 ama_____

2 ref_____

3 spec_____ *or* f_____

4 co_____

1b Label the pictures with words from above.

OK. I'll start the ball rolling. I love watching rugby. I go regularly to rugby matches all over the country. I never miss the home game of my local team, Northampton.

1 _____

I've been playing cricket all my life. Although I am now 39, I still play every Sunday. When I was 17, I was given the chance to play professional cricket but I wanted to go to university. There isn't a lot of money in professional cricket anyway, so I think I made a good choice.

2 _____

I've been training Trevor for the last six years and it was great news when he was chosen for the Olympics. Of course, it's sometimes hard because nobody really understands what we do, but when Trevor wins a gold medal, I'll know that I helped him get it.

3 _____

2 Match the idioms A–F with the correct paragraphs.

A scored an own goal   D be on the ball

B a whole new ball game   E take your eye off the ball

C a level playing field   F move the goalposts

1 I'm fed up with the behaviour of your representative. Every time we think we are near to making an agreement, he demands something else. If he continues to _____, we'll have to stop the negotiations.

2 My father retired ten years ago but last week he was asked to go back to the office to do some training. He says everything's changed now. The introduction of computers has made it _____.

3 If you want to pass your exams, you need to _____ and plan your revision carefully. Prepare well and you'll be fine.

4 I was going to buy the TV until the salesman _____ by telling me that he had the same model at home but it didn't have a good picture.

5 Make sure you ask the same questions in the speaking exams. We need to make sure there is _____ for all students.

6 If you are the manager, you can't _____ for one minute. One mistake could cost the company millions of pounds.

TRANSLATION

3 Translate the idioms from Exercise 2 into your own language. Can you say them the same way? If not, what do you say instead?

1 _____

2 _____

3 _____

4 _____

5 _____

6 _____

1a Underline words in the text where we can add *self-* in front of the word.

Why I love chess

Chess, for me, is the perfect sport to learn about your own limits and potential. It allows you to develop your control and your discipline. It is a game where concentration is very important and you must never show your enemy what you are thinking. As chess involves a lot of thinking and the use of logic, it aids your development. For example, I've read many chess books that have led me to read philosophy, history, etc. It also teaches you respect and confidence. I used to be shy and didn't believe in my own abilities. Now I am the life and soul of the party. Maybe chess doesn't teach you defence but did you know that for hundreds of years it was used to train army generals?

1b Use the words you underlined to describe these feelings.

1 I am on a diet so I'm not eating chocolate at the moment. *self-control*

2 I'm sure I can help you. _____

3 The thief tried to steal my wallet so I hit him.

_____

4 I'm learning a new language next semester.

_____

5 I must remember to take my pills every night.

_____

6 I'm very happy with my life and feel comfortable with myself. _____

2 Complete the sentences with the words in the box.

| courtesy | tolerance | coordination |
| flexibility | agility | calm |

1 If you want to play tennis, you must have good hand-eye _____ to be able to hit the ball every time.

2 I was amazed at his _____ when the judge told him that he would spend the rest of his life in prison.

3 My grandmother has incredible _____ for her age – she can still walk for miles.

4 The job requires a lot of _____ in your personal life as there are a lot of overseas business trips.

5 Our assistants have all been trained in _____ and should be polite to you at all times.

6 There will be no _____ of this type of behaviour and the guilty parties will be punished.

3a Tick the suffixes which are used to make nouns.

| -ly | -ion | -al | -ed | -ous | -ance | -ment |
| -ity | -ful | -ness | -ary | -ation | | |

3b Make nouns from these words using the correct suffix.

1 employ _____

2 thoughtless _____

3 appear _____

4 impress _____

5 imagine _____

6 domestic _____

7 digress _____

8 develop _____

9 elegant _____

10 helpful _____

PRONUNCIATION

4a Underline the main stress in these pairs of words.

1 agile – agility

2 tolerant – tolerance

3 confident - confidence

4 courteous – courtesy

5 coordinate – coordination

6 develop – development

7 flexible – flexibility

8 possible – possibility

4b `1.13` Listen and check your answers.

LISTENING

5 `1.14` Listen to a discussion on the topic 'Is chess a sport?' Tick the people who have similar opinions.

	Dr Smith	David Jones	Mrs Wilson
1 Chess is not a sport.			
2 It is recognised as a sport by many countries.			
3 It is an Olympic sport.			
4 It doesn't have much physical activity.			
5 It can be played on a computer.			
6 It has a world champion.			

GRAMMAR: quantifiers

6 `1.14` Listen again and tick the quantifiers that you hear.

none	almost none	hardly any	little
few	several some	much	lot of many
far too much	far too many	all	

7 Complete the text with the correct quantifiers. Sometimes more than one is possible.

Last month, [1]_____ of my friends – Steve, Jane, Peter and Sarah – asked me to set up a chess club. There are already [2]_____ clubs at the university (approximately 49). [3]_____ of them (almost 90 percent), in my opinion, are sports clubs. In fact there are [4]_____ games clubs. There's only the Bridge Club and the Scrabble Club.

However I've had a [5]_____ problems trying to set up this club. Firstly, there has been [6]_____ interest from students. So far, I've only received six emails in response to my invitation. Secondly, we would have to spend [7]_____ money to buy the equipment and rent the rooms. The university thinks we would need about £500.

In conclusion, I'm sorry to say that the chances of having a chess club are [8]_____ and I have decided to give up the idea.

8 Rewrite the sentences using a quantifer + *of*.

1 There are some friends of mine who are coming.

   Some *of my friends are coming.*

2 There are many boring programmes on TV.

   Many _____.

3 There are only a few computers that are ready.

   Few _____.

4 Not many teams will come this year.

   Hardly _____.

1 Read this 'Comment' from a sports magazine. Tick the sentence that best summarises the writer's opinion.

a) The writer thinks that, although Great Britain used to be good at hockey, it is now not very good. However, because there are so many teams now playing, it will get better.

b) The writer thinks that Great Britain is now not very good at hockey, even though it was the first country to play it. He thinks things won't get better until there are fewer teams. Until then the only chance for Great Britain is in mixed hockey.

c) The writer thinks that Great Britain cannot play any type of hockey very well. It has too many teams and not enough snow to be successful. It has no chance of winning medals now or at any time in the future.

A summary is a short version of a text that explains the main points. When trying to identify a good summary, identify the different points in the summary. Then find the place in the text where those points are talked about. Then check if the information in the summary and the text are the same. NOTE: You will, in the future, be asked to write summaries of a text. Remember, a summary only gives the main points, not all the information in a text.

2 Read the text again and decide if the statements are true or false.

1 The English invented football. ____

2 Great Britain has more hockey clubs than India. ____

3 The British have been more successful in ice hockey than grass hockey. ____

4 Grass hockey in Britain is not professional. ____

5 Most hockey clubs have more than three teams.

____

6 There is a lot of money in the sport. ____

7 The goalkeeper in mixed hockey must be a man. ____

8 Only Great Britain and the USA play mixed hockey.

____

HOW CAN WE GET BETTER AT HOCKEY?

I am not very <u>expert</u> at hockey but even I can see that there is something wrong. Grass hockey, or field hockey as the Americans like to call it, is another sport, like football, that the British invented and then stopped playing very well. In the men's game, Great Britain has only finished second once in the World Championships. In the women's game we have never finished in the first three. In terms of the Olympics we have one gold and one silver medal since 1952. It's true that the gold medal we won in 1982 in a <u>dramatic</u> final, was wonderful. Yet, that was nearly thirty years ago! It really is a <u>phenomenal</u> failure, even though only India and Pakistan have more hockey clubs than Great Britain.

So why is that we are so bad at hockey? It's true that we also invented ice hockey and any Briton has the right to feel <u>disgusted</u> by our complete failure in that. Maybe we are just not <u>aggressive</u> enough although any grass hockey player with a stick in their hand chasing after a ball looks pretty aggressive to me! Somehow, we English feel that grass hockey is more an English game than ice hockey. We'll leave that cold sport to countries that actually get some snow every year.

One reason that grass hockey has failed to achieve success for Great Britain is that we now live in the world of the <u>professional</u> sportsperson. Unlike ice hockey, grass hockey has remained an amateur sport. In the UK, thousands of people play. In fact you don't have to have any ability at all as most clubs have up to six teams playing hockey every Saturday or Sunday. Clubs that have so many teams don't have lots of people coming to watch games and don't charge money for tickets. They do not have the money to develop the game. With so little money in the sport there needs to be some focus on the better player. I think it should be made <u>illegal</u> for any club to have more than two or three teams. Then we might actually get better at the sport. Look at Holland, they only have a few teams and they are the best in the world!

Maybe the problem is that we're just no good with men and women's teams. And that's where Great Britain has a clever plan! In an <u>audacious</u> attempt to finally win a world championship in grass hockey, we have started promoting 'mixed' hockey. This is hockey played by a team of five women and five men. You can choose if you want a man or woman as goalkeeper. This is not a joke. In fact, mixed hockey is very common in the hockey world but most common here in Great Britain and the USA. What a surprise it is to hear that the UK Hockey Federation is now trying to organise the first Mixed Hockey World Championship. Wonderful! I look forward to lots of British gold medals!

3a Complete these sentences with the underlined words from the text on page 21.

1 At the age of seventeen he became a _____ footballer. He now earns a huge amount of money.

2 You need _____ advice about this. I suggest you speak to a lawyer.

3 How did he catch that ball? His jump was _____.

4 It was quite _____ of Steve to suggest that the Managing Director should resign.

5 I was _____ by the rude behaviour of your staff.

6 When he's angry he gets quite _____.

7 They should make smoking near babies _____.

8 It was a really _____ performance. I really didn't think she could win.

3b Write the noun forms of the adjectives above.

1 _____   5 _____

2 _____   6 _____

3 _____   7 _____

4 _____   8 _____

> ### GRAMMAR:
> ### definite and zero articles

4a Read the short text. Correct the six mistakes related to definite and zero articles.

> Field or grass hockey is similar to football as it is played by two teams of eleven players. ∧Two *The* teams will fight to control a ball and score goals. Here, though, there are some differences. For example, the ball that is used in hockey is much smaller than ball in football. Also, hockey uses the sticks instead of feet. Using a stick means you need to have the good coordination. Because of these sticks, hockey is considered to be one of most dangerous sports in the world. In England, hockey is usually taught at the school and there are over 5,000 clubs in the UK.

4b Match each correction with a reason why the definite or zero article needed to be used. There is one extra reason.

1 ___   2 ___   3 ___

4 ___   5 ___   6 ___

a) the noun is defined by a phrase that follows it

b) it is obvious from the context what we are referring to

c) we mention the noun a second time or use a substitute noun

d) we refer to something unique (including superlatives)

e) we focus on the type of institution rather than a particular or specific building

f) before plural nouns that are general, not specific

g) before abstract nouns

5 Complete the text with *the* or nothing.

I study at [1]_____ Warsaw University. I've been at [2]_____ university for three years. I've been playing in [3]_____ hockey team for two of those years. [4]_____ team is not very strong and we really only play for [5]_____ fun. [6]_____ matches we play, which are usually played on [7]_____ Saturdays, often mean we have to travel long distances. Last Saturday, to go to Poznan, we had to be at [8]_____ university by 7 a.m.! They have [9]_____ strongest team in Poland and we lost 10–0. [10]_____ journey home was not very happy.

READING

1 Read the two short texts and answer the questions.

1 Who broke a record? _____

2 Who won a medal? _____

3 Who was the oldest person at the time of their success? _____

1954: BANNISTER BREAKS FOUR-MINUTE MILE

Roger Bannister, a 25-year-old British medical student, has become the first man to run a mile in less than four minutes. His time was 3 minutes 59.4 seconds, achieved at the Iffley Road track in Oxford and watched by about 3,000 spectators.

1952: ZATOPEK WINS GOLD AT HELSINKI

30 year-old Emil Zatopek of Czechoslovakia has won the 10,000 metre race one day after the 15th Olympic Games opened at Helsinki, Finland.

KEY LANGUAGE: emphasis and comparison

2 Write these words under the correct heading.

tremendous	incredible	extremely
incredibly	totally	undoubtedly	truly
definitely	amazing	particularly
extraordinary	impressive

Adjectives	Adverbs

3 [1.15] Listen to three journalists discussing great moments in athletics history. Tick the adjectives and adverbs from Exercise 2 that you hear.

4 [1.15] Listen again and answer these questions.

1 What is the topic of the article?

_____

2 How long did Roger Bannister keep his record?

_____

3 How many gold medals did Emil Zatopek win at the Helsinki Olympics?

_____

4 Who will give the presentation?

_____

5a Complete the presentation with phrases of emphasis and comparison.

For our article next month, we've decided to go with Emil Zatopek. That he was a tremendous athlete is certain. There's no ¹_____. However, there is one competition that particularly shows Emil to ²_____ be one of the greatest athletes in history. That was the 1952 Olympics in Helsinki. By the time of the marathon, Emil had already won the 10,000 metres and 5,000 metres and in both events he broke Olympic records. Any great athlete would have been ³_____ by then, but not Emil. ⁴_____, about Emil is that he had never run a marathon before the Olympics. But he didn't only win the marathon. What ⁵_____ was that he won it easily and again broke the Olympic record.

At a time when it was difficult to follow the whole race, imagine the faces of the spectators when Emil ran into the stadium to complete the marathon. Everyone in the stadium must have known they were watching an ⁶_____ in athletics history. But, ⁷_____, since 1952 no one has repeated Emil's achievement.

5b [1.16] Listen and check your answers.

STUDY SKILLS: understanding essay questions

1 Complete these essay questions with a suitable word or phrase.

1 'Love is more important than money.' _____.

2 _____ for the increase in temperature over the last few years.

3 _____ in detail the steps taken in your final experiment of the semester, and the results of the experiment.

4 Compare _____ the choices open to the Senate for next year's budget and make recommendations.

5 To _____ was his stay in Ireland influential to Johnson's writing?

6 _____ the reasons why working from home is better than working in an office.

7 Briefly _____ the decisions taken by the government over the last five months to improve environmental conditions.

DICTATION

2 **1.17** Listen and write the introduction to a 'for and against' essay.

'Billionaires are destroying football'. Discuss.

_____

_____

_____

_____

_____

_____

WRITING SKILLS: 'for and against' essays

3 Tick any of the following that are present in the introduction in Exercise 2.

opinion ☐

the aim/target of the essay ☐

arguments and examples ☐

a context for the question ☐

4 Read the rest of the essay. Match phrases a–g with gaps 1–7.

a) in contrast

b) in conclusion

c) in simple terms

d) many people argue

e) firstly

f) on balance

g) it is also clear that

It is true that some of these billionaires know nothing of football but others do. In fact there seem to be two types of billionaire owners. ¹___, there are those who really love football, such as Mr Gaydamak of Portsmouth. Then there are those who are interested in the club as a business, such as the new owners of Manchester United. ²___ that these billionaires are destroying the game. The owners are only interested in short-term success and spend money to achieve this. ³___, this means that they buy expensive foreign players rather than spend time improving the quality of British players. This means that the English national team suffers.

⁴___, people can say that the quality of football has improved in England. This has also resulted in more interest in English football at home and abroad. ⁵___ footballers now want to play in England, rather than Italy or Spain.

⁶___, there are arguments for and against rich billionaires buying football teams in England. ⁷___, I believe it is a good thing because the interest in English football provides more money which can then be used to improve the quality of English footballers.

4 Medicine

4.1 MEDICAL BREAKTHROUGHS

1 Fill the gaps in the text with one word. The first letter(s) are given to help you.

Health Centre Newsletter

December 2008

Unfortunately the pharmacist's office has had to close. This means that the Health Centre will no longer provide ¹ an_____ or ² pa_____. There is a pharmacy on the High Street which will supply you with what you need. Please remember to always have your prescription with you.

Although the pharmacy here has closed, the Health Centre will continue to give ³ i_____ for people over the age of 65 who suffer from ⁴ di_____ and/ or ⁵ ar_____.

There are some changes to the staff here at the Health Centre. We'd like to welcome a new member to the team. Melanie Sykes is our new ⁶ m_____. She is hoping to run her first course for pregnant mothers next week and will start visiting the week after. At the same time, we are sorry to say goodbye to Dr Tellman, who intends to continue his studies to become a ⁷ s_____. He is particularly interested in learning to do ⁸ tr_____ for sufferers of heart ⁹ d_____.

Finally, a reminder for elderly patients. Be especially careful of getting a ¹⁰ c_____ infection at this time of the year.

2a Complete the table.

Subject/Place	Person
biology	
psychology	
	pharmacist
radiology	
	ecologist
physiotherapy	
psychiatry	

2b Correct the rule.

Many nouns that end with -e are a subject or discipline, e.g. *biology*. When we talk about the people who do or practise this subject or discipline, we often drop the -e and add the suffix -er.

NOTE Not all words describing people end in -ist, e.g. *historian*, used to describe someone who is interested in history.

3 Match words from Exercise 2a with these definitions.

1 Someone who is interested in how people think.

_____ or _____

2 The use of X-rays, for example. _____

3 Exercising to help you recover from injuries or operations. _____

4 Someone who studies how people, plants and animals are related to the environment. _____

1 Correct each sentence by replacing the word in bold with one of the others.

1 Keep indoors out of the cold or you might get an **anaesthetist**, like a sore throat. _infection_

2 There are many different types of **parasite** which can affect your heart, lungs, kidneys or other parts of your body. For many, there is still no cure.

3 He's got a **vaccine**. We need to bring his temperature down.

4 There is still no **contracted** for Dengue Fever.

5 Does he have any of the **cancer** of the disease?

6 He **fever** malaria when he was on holiday in Africa.

7 Before your operation you will see the **infection** to make sure you don't feel a thing.

8 The **symptoms** gets into your blood and affects the whole body.

Killer mosquito disease arrives in Europe
06 September 2007

A TROPICAL DISEASE that has caused illness and significant panic on the islands of the Indian Ocean has appeared in Europe for the first time.
   ¹____ A total of 151 cases were reported in two villages near the town of Cervia between 4 July and 3 September. Eleven patients were taken to hospital; one died.
   ²____ The disease is transmitted by one particular type, the *Aedes albopictus* which is common in southern Europe and has been found as far north as Belgium. It is the first time this disease has been detected in Europe and raises the threat that the risk of infection could increase in other countries, including the UK.
   ³____ In addition, there is no vaccine or way to immunise oneself against the disease. They warned travellers to Emilia Romagna to protect themselves against mosquitoes. Pregnant women and those with chronic illnesses were urged to seek medical advice before visiting the area.

2 Read the text and match sentences a–c with gaps 1–3.

a) The European Centre for Disease Control and Prevention (ECDC) yesterday confirmed that, like malaria, there is no treatment for Chikungunya disease.

b) The Ministry of Health in Italy has confirmed an outbreak of Chikungunya disease near Ravenna in the region of Emilia Romagna, 200 miles north of Rome.

c) Like malaria, Chikungunya is carried by the mosquito.

3 Tick the sentence(s) which the writer agrees with.

1 This is the first time we have heard about this disease.

2 The disease has previously been seen in Europe.

3 This disease is carried and given to people by insects.

4 There is no danger that this disease will spread to the UK.

5 As yet there is no cure for the disease.

6 People should avoid the area completely until the virus is under control.

MALARIA

LISTENING

4 [1.18] Listen to a medical team preparing for a research trip to Emilia Romagna. Tick the activities that you hear.

meet to form teams ☐

fill in questionnaires ☐

treat patients ☐

collect insects ☐

collect blood samples ☐

test the new vaccines ☐

give boosters ☐

do nothing ☐

continue working on the new vaccines in the lab ☐

try to find a cure ☐

bring patients from Italy ☐

show the results of the research ☐

find some people who know about mosquitoes ☐

GRAMMAR: future continuous, *going to*, present continuous

5 [1.18] Listen again. Look at the activities you ticked in Exercise 4. Which future form did the speaker use? Number the activities 1, 2 or 3. Check your answers in the audioscript on page 90.

1 future continuous

2 *going to*

3 present continuous

6 Add one extra word in each sentence, if it is needed.

   won't

1 We ⋀ be doing anything more on the project until your return.

2 Will you taking Sarah to the wedding?

3 The government going to make a decision by the end of next week.

4 We aren't going to get a car because we don't have the money.

5 They won't be recruiting any new people this year.

6 I seeing the psychiatrist this Friday.

7 I'm going return this book to the library tomorrow.

8 I'm taking my children to the circus tonight.

7 Rewrite the sentences using either the future continuous, *going to* or the present continuous of the verb in brackets.

1 Before you go on holiday, is it your intention to have an injection for malaria? (have)

Before you go on holiday, *are you going to have an injection for malaria?*

2 My appointment with the doctor is for Monday at 10.30 a.m. (see)

I _____.

3 I'm going home now and then travelling to my parents' to stay for the rest of the week. (stay)

From tomorrow, _____.

4 When I've finished the report, I want to take a break. (take)

When _____.

5 Have you arranged to meet Peter this weekend? (meet)

Are _____?

6 The midwife is arranging check-ups for all our expectant mothers throughout next week. (give)

The _____.

7 I want to see the exhibition before it closes on Friday. (see)

I _____.

8 The cleaners take the first bus just for this week. (arrive)

The cleaners _____.

TRANSLATION

8 Translate these words into your own language. Are any of them similar in your own language?

1 symptom _____

2 infection _____

3 contract _____

4 fever _____

5 vaccine _____

6 parasite _____

7 cancer _____

8 anaesthetist _____

DICTATION

1 **1.19** Listen to the task given to a group of university students. Write down what you hear.

_____

_____

_____

_____

_____

_____

READING

2 Read the extract on cosmetic surgery. Are these comments true, false or not given in the text?

1 More men want cosmetic surgery than women.

2 Men compare themselves to other men in adverts.

3 Cosmetic surgery is too expensive for most people.

4 More men than ever are not looking after their health.

5 Women are encouraging their partners to have cosmetic surgery.

6 There need to be laws to control who can open a clinic and who can work in one.

7 There are many cases of cosmetic surgery that have gone wrong.

8 Drug companies are also making money from cosmetic surgery.

GRAMMAR: future perfect, *will*

3 Underline the following in the text.

1 four examples of *will* + adverbs of certainty

2 two examples of the future perfect

4 Look at the chart. Write sentences using either *will* or the future perfect.

	In the future …		By 2050 …
1	discovery of cures for cancer and Alzheimer's	5	many parts of the world run out of food
2	huge increase in poverty	6	population reach over 10 billion
3	people healthier	7	transplants become cheap enough for everyone
4	disappearance of more animals from the world	8	average age increase to over 75

1 _____

2 _____

3 _____

4 _____

5 _____

6 _____

7 _____

8 _____

THE PRICE OF MALE BEAUTY

It seems that millions of men still think their bodies can be saved – with cosmetic surgery. In the next year, almost half of all men will probably take no regular exercise and eat appallingly, a survey commissioned for *The Sunday Telegraph* has revealed. Yet a staggering 25 percent said they will possibly have surgery to improve their looks.

However, experts have warned that a 'quick fix' culture is taking hold, with men pinning their hopes on cosmetic tricks while taking no steps to secure basic levels of health, and by the end of the decade we will have seen a major decrease in the health levels of men as a whole.

It is also clear that not everyone approves of male cosmetic surgery. A lot of women said that they could not adjust to the idea of their partner or husband having cosmetic surgery. However, it seems that men have as much pressure put on them as women to participate in this new trend. For example, beautiful men selling anything from aftershave to underpants can be seen wherever you look. *Men's Health* magazine has stated that this barrage of images of 'perfection' will certainly result in a rush of men desperate to go under

the knife. This is great news not only for the surgeons but also for pharmaceutical companies who are finding the business of cosmetic surgery very profitable indeed.

However, the industry is still not regulated and there are many clinics appearing with doctors and surgeons who are inexperienced and under-qualified. By the end of the year, clinics will have completed over 35,000 cosmetic procedures in the UK alone. Ten percent of those procedures will almost certainly be at low-quality clinics. A recent investigation by the Metropolitan Police resulted in the closure of five clinics and three surgeons going to prison.

VOCABULARY: dependent prepositions

5 Choose the correct preposition a, b, c or d.

1 People will have to learn to adjust ___ the changing conditions in the environment.

   a) to   b) on   c) in   d) with

2 I don't think I approve ___ parents smoking.

   a) with   b) to   c) of   d) over

3 His parents have to consent ___ the transplant.

   a) on   b) with   c) over   d) to

4 Doctors need to be able to relate ___ their patients.

   a) with   b) to   c) in   d) on

5 I would like you to participate ___ the consultation.

   a) over   b) on   c) in   d) of

6 Have you succeeded ___ convincing them?

   a) to   b) in   c) on   d) with

READING

READ BETTER

When looking for specific information in a text, first identify what you are looking for. If you are answering questions, underline the key words. When you read, you should look for synonyms or words of similar meaning to the words you have underlined. Read the whole text quickly, underlining where you think the information is and then read the underlined sections more carefully. In a task like Exercise 6 there will usually only be one answer for each section.

6 Read the extracts from interviews with people about cosmetic surgery. Which person (A–F) …

1 thinks cosmetic surgery is a waste of money? ___

2 thinks people want to be better than each other? ___

3 thinks cosmetic surgery helps his career? ___

4 thinks cosmetic surgery won't improve your health? ___

5 found that cosmetic surgery didn't help him? ___

6 thinks that men don't decide – women do? ___

A I read all about this. I can understand why people want quick solutions like plastic surgery, but in fact procedures like liposuction have no health benefits at all. Staying beautiful while sitting in front of my TV sounds nice, but I'd rather earn it by spending time down the gym.

B It's not our fault! I hate to say it, but women are putting pressure on men. They want us to look like the guy from the Calvin Klein advert. Look at me. What chance have I got? You hear about women getting cosmetic surgery as birthday presents. Soon our wives will be giving similar birthday presents to us!

C It's the whole 'Keeping Up with the Jones's' thing. If the woman next door has it, then your wife wants it. Well now it's men. Do we want to be the same as everyone else or different? It's a matter of choice as to how far people will go to fit into the pressures of society. Me, I like the way I am.

D I've actually had an operation. I'm not getting any younger and I'm a bit of a sucker for the ladies. To be honest, it hasn't made any difference. It can change your looks but it can't change your character. I'm still old and boring!

E For people like me it's really important. There is a pressure on jobs and general appearance in the City. The ravages of life catch up – people work late, travel long distances and entertain clients. It shows on the face. Last year I broke my nose in a football match. The next week I lost a contract and someone suggested that I didn't look like someone who could be trusted … because of my broken nose. I soon sorted that problem out.

F I think it's funny. I don't understand why we women need cosmetic surgery, let alone men! I get old with my husband. I like it like that. Personally I think it should be banned and the money spent on really sick people.

VOCABULARY: adverbs of certainty

1a Complete the adverbs of certainty.

1 ce_____

2 pr_____

3 un_____

4 po_____

5 de_____

1b Complete the sentences with the adverbs above. More than one adverb may be correct.

1 I will _____ ask for an increase in our budget next year, but it will depend how much money we spend on research next month.

2 He will _____ agree. I can guarantee that.

3 There will _____ be some disadvantages. I'm sure of it.

4 There will _____ be an opportunity to take the exams next year, but I think it unlikely.

5 _____ there will be people who will criticise you. There always are.

PRONUNCIATION

2 `1.20` Listen to these sentences. Are the adverbs of certainty stressed or not?

1 It could possibly happen at any time.

2 There will definitely be psychological effects.

3 He will certainly complete it on time.

3 `1.21` Practise saying these sentences. Then listen and check if you are putting the stress in the right place.

1 The operation will probably take place this afternoon.

2 I will certainly let you know when I have an answer.

3 This is undoubtedly the right decision.

EXTRA VOCABULARY: adverbs of certainty as answers

4 Adverbs of certainty can also be used on their own, as answers to questions. Answer these questions with the correct adverb.

1 A: Can I see my mother tomorrow?

   B: _____. I'll take you to her at 8 a.m.

2 A: Will they agree to the proposal?

   B: _____. They know they have no choice.

3 A: Is there a chance of the meeting still going ahead?

   B: _____. However, I doubt it.

4 A: Will we be able to carry out the transplant?

   B: _____. I'd say there's an 80 percent chance.

KEY LANGUAGE: predicting

5 One sentence in each dialogue is incorrect. Correct it.

1 A: Perhaps we can spend the money on some new books?

   B: No, I think the board will be wanting us to spend it on improving the facilities.

   _____

2 A: I don't know how we're going to get this plan approved.

   B: Well, I talk to Sue Green tomorrow afternoon – she's on the planning board – so I'll see what I can do.

   _____

3 A: What's the opinion of the doctors doing his cosmetic surgery?

   B: They think it give him a very different outlook on life.

   _____

4 A: I don't know what to think about this new law. It could bad for our competitors but good for us.

   B: Yes, we need to see how things develop.

   _____

1 Match headings 1–4 with example sentences a–d.

1 Conclusion   3 Recommendations

2 Facts and Findings   4 Introduction

a) More nurses should be employed as soon as possible.

b) To sum up, there are not enough nurses to look after the number of patients in the hospital.

c) This report looks at the role of nurses at the County Hospital.

d) The average nurse is now working 17 hours a day.

READING

2 Match headings 1–4 in Exercise 1 with gaps a–d in the report.

3 Read the report and answer the questions.

1 What is the report about?

_____

2 How many recommendations are made?

_____

3 How many facts and findings are there?

_____

4 How many sources did the writer use?

_____

5 Is the conclusion positive or negative?

_____

4 1.22 Listen to a presentation of the report and fill in gaps 1–9.

5 Put the words in the correct order to make other recommendations.

1 be changed address web could the

_____

2 advertise good be the website idea to might a it

_____

3 that hospital the its a responsibility patients it has understand must to

_____

4 essential references is people's check to it

_____

 St Swithin's Hospital

REPORT FOR THE HOSPITAL BOARD

a ____

This report investigates St Swithin's hospital website. It includes recommendations for the hospital.

The report gathered information from the following sources:

- the website itself.
- its links to other websites.
- the opinions of 1_____.

b ____

- It is not clear what the purpose of the website is. Is it for 2_____, for doctors and surgeons to publish their articles, or to supply a link for Internet shopping?
- There are too many links to irrelevant websites.
- It hasn't been updated for 3_____.
- It doesn't show that there are well-known doctors and surgeons working at the hospital.
- The website is run by two doctors, one of whom 4_____.

c ____

This is a poor website and something 5_____.

d ____

1 It 6_____ for the hospital to hire a professional company to recreate the website.

2 It 7_____ the hospital prepares a clear description of what they want on the website.

3 The hospital 8_____ that the old website cannot continue and therefore it 9_____ immediately.

5 Transport

5.1 GETTING FROM A TO B

DICTATION

1 ⬜1.23 Listen and write what you hear.

_____

_____

_____

_____

VOCABULARY: methods of transport

2a Tick which type of transport is being described in Exercise 1.

balloon	coach	ferry	helicopter
lorry/truck	maglev train	motorbike	
scooter	submarine	tram	van

2b Label the following definitions of types of transport using some of the words above.

1 A vehicle which is not very powerful or fast and has two small wheels. _____

2 A type of aircraft with large metal blades on top which turn around very quickly to make it fly.

_____

3 A ship, usually military, that can stay under water.

_____

4 A boat that carries people and things across water.

_____

5 A large bag with gas and a basket for passengers.

_____

6 A large vehicle for carrying heavy goods. _____

7 A small fast two-wheeled vehicle with an engine.

_____

8 A bus with comfortable seats used for long journeys. _____

9 A vehicle which uses metal tracks in the street.

_____

VOCABULARY: transport problems

3 Complete the types of transport problems. Some letters have been given to help you.

1 _ _ _ tide

2 turb _ _ _ _ _ _

3 sign _ _ _ _ _ _   pr _ _ _ _ _ _ _

4 punc _ _ _ _ _

5 tail _ _ _ _ _

6 fogb _ _ _ _   r _ _ _ _ _ _

7 rou _ _   w _ _ _ _ _ _ _

8 la _ _ _   clo _ _ _ _ _

9 plat _ _ _ _ _   alte _ _ _ _ _ _ _ _

VOCABULARY: safety features

4 Read the text. Put the underlined safety features in the correct place.

For the last few years the police have tried everything to reduce road accidents. New laws requiring the use of [1] one-way both in the front seat and the back seat have been passed. [2] Speed cameras to help the driver control the car better have been made compulsory in all cars, as have [3] traffic lights in both the front seats, but not in the back seat because they may be dangerous for small children. More [4] seat belts have been installed at main crossroads. [5] Anti-lock brakes have been made lower so that they are easier to break. [6] Speed limits have been put up, but these have proved to be very expensive and people have started vandalising the cameras. Streets are now [7] airbags in many city centres to make traffic more manageable. Yet still the rate of deaths has not decreased.

TRANSLATION

5 Translate these types of transport into your own language.

1 cable car _____   4 hovercraft _____

2 glider _____   5 quad bike _____

3 hydrofoil _____   6 barge _____

READING

1 Read the text and complete the table.

Type of transport	Gap	Will it be used: probable/not probable
Solar sail		
Teleportation		
Flying cars		
Slidewalk		

2 Read the text again. Are these sentences true, false or not given?

1 Eventually there will be no fossil fuel.

2 Science fiction cannot help us predict the future of transport.

3 One form of transport will be very expensive.

4 One form of transport may be dangerous for humans.

5 One form of transport will help buildings fly.

6 Tracks can travel anywhere.

7 New types of roads and motorways will be built.

8 One form of transport relies on power from space.

9 All of the forms of transport use a type of power other than fossil fuel.

Science fiction
transport for the future

What are the possibilities for transport in the future? Today, most of the vehicles we use are driven by fossil fuels, but we won't be able to use fossil fuels forever. What are we going to do when they run out?

Writers of science fiction have written a lot on this subject and although many people might think that their ideas are too fantastic to ever happen, the truth is actually not so clear. Let's look at a few of those 'science fiction' methods of transport and find out if anyone is actually taking them seriously.

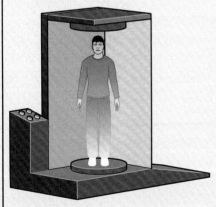

With ¹_____, people and things will be able to move from one place to another almost instantaneously. People won't have to move at all. However, some scientists believe it might result in the destruction of the human being.

Experiments have been carried out and there has been some success in moving atoms and groups of atoms, but we are a long way away from moving objects or humans. We might never know if this form of transport will actually work.

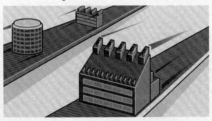

A ²_____ is like a flat escalator except that it will have tracks all over the country and will be so strong that it will be able to move very fast and hold buildings. Unfortunately, it will have to be very strong indeed, and until today, there is no evidence that anything would be strong enough to carry such weight and move fast. In addition, scientists believe anything with tracks won't be able to carry people everywhere.

A ³_____ would take power from the sun and use this power to transport people and things with the use of large mirrors. This seems particularly good for space travel as the vehicle won't need to be regularly filled up. After all, the sun shines all the time in space. It is

already in use, but at the moment scientists think it is impractical to build large versions and further experimentation will have to wait for the future.

If we have ⁴_____, we won't need to build roads or motorways as everyone will be able to travel above ground rather than on the ground. Currently there are many projects, and prototypes might be produced in the next ten years. However, it fails to deal with one issue – that in a hundred years we might not have any fuel to use these vehicles. There is no evidence as yet that this form of transport will be able to use an alternative form of power to work.

GRAMMAR: modal verbs (future)

3 Look at the text on page 33. Find examples of the following.

able to   might

have to   need to

4 Underline the correct future modal forms in the text.

Let's have a look at our problems for the coming year. We definitely won't ¹ *have to / be able to / need to* enlarge our fleet of lorries because we won't have enough money. This means that we will ² *have to / might / be able to* continue with just six trucks. Vasco Co ³ *might / have to / need to* be able to lend us four lorries but this will depend on how much work they have. As for drivers, we will ⁴ *might / need to / be able to* replace Michael Kowalski as he is returning to Poland. Lisa has had her baby and although she says she wants to come back, she ⁵ *won't be able to / won't need to / might not* return after maternity leave. We'll ⁶ *be able to / have to / might* wait and see. I'm hoping Steve will ⁷ *be able to / need to / might* cover for her. If not, we will ⁸ *might / be able to / have to* find two new drivers. However, if the first three months of the year go well, we ⁹ *need to / might / have to* be able to employ another driver and then we will ¹⁰ *might / be able to / need to* buy another truck.

5 Complete the second sentence so that it has a similar meaning to the first sentence. Use the word in bold in the future form and other words. Use between two and five words.

1 The car has been fixed so it's possible we will go tomorrow.
might
The car has been fixed so *we might go* tomorrow.

2 It will be necessary to buy my own car when I retire next year.
have to
I _____ my own car when I retire next year.

3 I passed my exams so I can have the summer free.
need
Because I passed my exams, _____ attend the summer course.

4 From next week, it won't be possible for children to enter the pool on their own.
able
From next week, children _____ enter the pool on their own.

5 It's not possible to wear jeans in the theatre.
can't
You _____ in the theatre.

6 Is there a chance we can meet Tom Cruise when he visits?
able to
_____ meet Tom Cruise when he visits?

7 It is possible you will have to wait until I can find you a table.
may
You _____ until I can find you a table.

VOCABULARY: words connected with transport

6 Complete the sentences with the words in the box.

| tycoon | fleet | masses | emits | fumes |
| feasible | elevated | freight | shuttle | |

1 It's so crowded! There are _____ of people here!

2 This car alarm _____ a very loud sound that will attract people from more than a mile away.

3 A large _____ of fishing boats leaves the port every morning at 4.30 a.m.

4 Our guest speaker will talk from an _____ platform so everyone can see him.

5 Your proposals are just not _____. We don't have that much money.

6 Our lorries carry _____ between Paris and London.

7 We had to empty the laboratory because of chemical _____ created by the experiment.

8 Yet another football team has been bought by a _____.

9 I'll take the _____ to the centre of town and then walk to the office from there.

5.3

VOCABULARY: words from the lesson

1 Complete the text with the words in the box.

era	nostalgia	gruelling	altitude
impeccable	nomads	icon	opulence

BOOKS TO READ: AROUND THE WORLD IN EIGHTY DAYS

Jules Verne's classic novel, published in 1873 is still a great novel to read. The period when Verne was writing was an ¹_____ of great technological breakthroughs, particularly in the world of transport. For the first time, it was possible to actually travel round the world in relative comfort and safety, and if you had the money, in some ²_____. In the novel, Phileas Fogg, a typical English gentleman of ³_____ manners, accepts a bet to travel round the world in just eighty days. The whole novel describes this ⁴_____ journey on boats and trains and what life was like in the cities. Phileas does not see any ⁵_____ living in deserts and does not climb to the high ⁶_____ of the Himalayas. However, for nineteenth-century readers, the novel was still a fantastic adventure, describing places that few people had ever seen.

One interesting point is that the image of Phileas in a balloon has become an ⁷_____ of the novel. However, Phileas rejects the idea of flying in a balloon in the book. Balloon or no balloon, reading *Around the World in Eighty Days* today, we are filled with a sense of ⁸_____ for a world now disappeared, where life seemed simpler and more exciting.

PENGUIN CLASSICS

JULES VERNE

Around the World in Eighty Days

LISTENING

2 `1.24` Listen to the first part of a talk and choose the best answer a, b or c to complete the sentences.

1 The talk is about …
  a) a famous book.
  b) how a book was adapted for TV.
  c) how a book was made into a film.

2 The character in the novel …
  a) didn't use modern forms of travel.
  b) was able to finish his journey on time.
  c) couldn't succeed because there were no planes.

3 Michael Palin was able to …
  a) use his own choice of transport.
  b) use only similar transport to Jules Verne.
  c) use only similar transport to Phileas Fogg.

Michael Palin

3 `1.25` Listen to the second part of the talk and answer the question.

How many countries are mentioned in the second half of the talk?

4a Tick the types of transport that Michael Palin uses on his journey.

dog sled ☐

train ☐

car ☐

coach/bus ☐

coach and horses ☐

plane ☐

balloon ☐

ship ☐

motorbike ☐

4b `1.25` Listen again and check.

GRAMMAR:
modal verbs (past)

---

5 Complete the sentences with past modal verbs. Check your answers in the audioscript on page 91.

1 An English gentleman _____ travelling around the world.

2 Michael _____ use planes and cars but _____ use trains and ships instead.

3 Palin _____ use modern forms of transport but _____ use any form of transport that was available to Phileas Fogg.

4 Palin started on the Orient Express and _____ get off until he was in Austria.

5 He _____ get out of Austria by coach.

6 He _____ make his connection to Saudi Arabia.

7 Palin _____ make up all the lost time.

6 Rewrite the sentences using past modal verbs from the box.

```
could    couldn't    was able to    wasn't able to
managed to    succeeded in    didn't have to
wasn't allowed to    had to
```

1 My mother didn't let me go out after dark.

   I _____.

---

2 It was necessary for me to get a student card when I arrived at the university.

   I _____.

3 The bus didn't arrive on time today because of snow blocking the roads.

   The bus _____.

4 Although there was a lot of disagreement, the government did pass the law.

   The government _____.

5 When I was younger I ran a mile in five minutes.

   When I _____.

6 After a lot of pushing, they finally opened the door.

   They _____.

PRONUNCIATION

7a `1.26` Listen to these sentences. Underline the two words in each sentence that are joined together.

1 He <u>had to</u> leave early.

2 He managed to arrive on time.

3 They succeeded in changing trains.

4 There were able to arrange it.

5 He was allowed to stay.

7b In which of the sentences is one sound not pronounced? Which sound is it?

8 `1.27` Practise saying these verb phrases, joining the words together.

1 managed to

2 succeeded in

3 was able to

4 allowed to

5 had to

6 didn't have to

7 wasn't able to

1 Complete the sentences with the words in the box.

doubt answer surely essential way forward really agree solution that best way sure

a But I _____ think that we've made some progress.

b I think the best _____ would be to spend another week on safety tests …

c Don't you think _____ the brakes have improved in testing?

d Yet, it's _____ to remember our responsibility to the drivers of our cars.

e That's the _____ to go for now.

f But _____ you can't argue that it's ready to go on the road?

g It's the _____ for us.

h But I'm _____ you can see that we can only put this car on the market when we are sure it's safe.

i There's no _____ in my mind, Janosz that the tests have been a failure.

j But you must _____ that wasn't our fault!

k I think the _____ is to postpone tests …

2a Match sentences a–k in Exercise 1 with gaps 1–11.

MURAT: ¹___ The car still isn't ready to drive. ²___ and go back to the laboratory.

JANOSZ: I'm not so sure, Murat. ³___ They were much worse in earlier tests.

MURAT: Yes, that's true. ⁴___ The test dummy went straight through the window!

JANOSZ: ⁵___ David forgot to put the seat belt on the dummy!

MURAT: Did he? I didn't know. ⁶___ Can you really say it's safe right now?

JANOSZ: To be honest, no. ⁷___ Remember how hopeless we felt last week? Testing is the key. ⁸___

MURAT: Yes. We have made progress. ⁹___ They must feel safe. OK, ¹⁰___ and then decide.

JANOSZ: I agree. ¹¹___

2b 1.28 Listen and check your answers.

1 Label the charts, graphs and tables.

A _____

Type of transport used by people in Europe to go to work

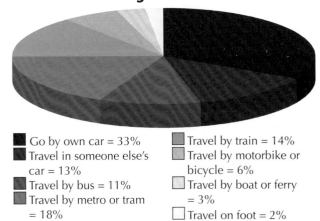

■ Go by own car = 33%
■ Travel in someone else's car = 13%
■ Travel by bus = 11%
■ Travel by metro or tram = 18%

■ Travel by train = 14%
■ Travel by motorbike or bicycle = 6%
□ Travel by boat or ferry = 3%
□ Travel on foot = 2%

B _____

Preferred method of transport in Europe 1995 / 2000 / 2005 (in thousands)

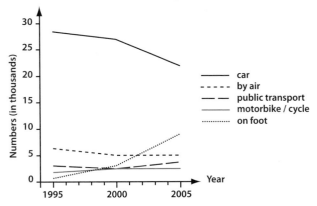

—— car
- - - by air
– – public transport
—— motorbike / cycle
······ on foot

C _____

How often a typical family in Manchester (the Smiths) uses transport in a month

	Week 1	Week 2	Week 3	Week 4
car	★★★★★★★	★★★★★★★	★★★★★★★	★★★★★★★★★★★★
public transport (e.g. bus, metro, tram, ferry)	★★★	★	★★	
motorbike / bicycle	★			
on foot	★★★★★★★★★	★★★★★★★★★★	★★★★★★★★★★★	★★★★★★★

2 Read the following information. Match it with A, B or C in Exercise 1.

In 1995 the car was the most popular means of transport. [1] On the other hand, the car remained the most popular means of transport in 2000 and 2005. [2] Moreover, between 1995 and 2005 the number of people preferring the car decreased. In 1995 the second most preferred method of transport was by air, [3] similarly by 2005 it had been replaced by travelling on foot. One might have expected travelling on foot would decrease over the ten years but it actually increased. [4] Whereas, it increased by 800 percent. The preference for public transport decreased between 1995 and 2000. [5] While, between 2000 and 2005 the preference for public transport actually increased, [6] however the preference for air travel stayed the same.

3 The underlined words and phrases in Exercise 2 are in the wrong place. Put them in the right order.

1 *Similarly*

2 _____

3 _____

4 _____

5 _____

6 _____

WRITE BETTER

When identifying the correct use of words and rearranging words, you may make the task easier by seeing whether there is a comma after the word or not. Some words always have a comma after them. Some words nearly always have a comma before them.

4 Answer the questions.

1 Which words and phrases in the text always have a comma after them?

_____

2 Which words and phrases in the text usually have a comma before them?

_____

5 Complete the report about the pie chart on page 37.

This is a description of [1]_____ people in Europe use to go to work. The [2]_____ is the car. There was a large difference [3]_____ and other forms of transport. For example, the car was chosen by 33 percent of respondents, [4]_____ popular means of transport, the metro or tram, was only 18 percent. This is [5]_____ with the difference between [6]_____ and travelling by train, where the difference is only 1 percent. People may have expected travelling on foot to be very popular. [7]_____, it only received 2 percent. [8]_____, travelling by boat or ferry wasn't very popular.

6 Use the reports in Exercises 2 and 5 to write a description about the remaining table.

_____

_____

_____

_____

_____

_____

_____

_____

_____

_____

_____

_____

_____

_____

_____

_____

_____

_____

_____

_____

6 Literature

6.1 THE NOBEL PRIZE

VOCABULARY: literature

1a Match the type of writing 1–12 with the most appropriate writer a–g. Use 'author' when there is no one clear choice.

> a poet   b dramatist   c novelist
> d biographer   e critic   f ghostwriter
> g author

1 memoirs g
2 blogs ____
3 poetry ____
4 travel writing ____
5 autobiographies ____
6 biographies ____
7 novels ____
8 plays ____
9 diaries ____
10 essays ____
11 history ____
12 thriller ____

1b Complete the text with words from above.

Wendell Jones has certainly had an interesting life, working in government over the last 25 years. During the time, he kept a collection of ¹_____, which he wrote in every day. Now, he has used this collection to put together his ²_____ of his time in government. He told me that he had thought of writing an ³_____ but he didn't have the time and didn't trust a ⁴_____ to do it for him.

At times, the book reads like a ⁵_____ with all the secret meetings and people talking behind each other's back. It certainly will keep you interested! Of course, the ⁶_____ hated it but you should be the judge and decide yourself. Personally I loved it.

If you want to discuss this book further, come to my ⁷_____ at www.sallyann.co.uk.

VOCABULARY: words from the lesson

2 Write + (usually positive) or – (usually negative) after each adjective.

1 awful
2 disturbing
3 dull
4 gripping
5 lightweight
6 overrated
7 shocking
8 brilliant
9 dreadful
10 exciting
11 interesting
12 moving
13 tedious
14 thought-provoking

3 Rewrite the sentences so that they have a similar meaning. Use the phrases in the box.

> lived up to the hype   a real let-down
> couldn't put it down   not my kind of thing
> easy to read   couldn't get into it
> hard-going at the beginning   a real page-turner

1 I read it in one afternoon without stopping.

   I _couldn't put it down._

2 My friends told me it was great but I thought it was rubbish.

   I thought it was _____.

3 It started badly but got better after 20 pages.

   It was _____.

4 It's a history novel. I prefer science fiction.

   It's _____.

5 Just when you think you know everything, something else happens and you want to read more.

   It's _____.

6 It has a lot of information in it, but it is clearly written and I understood everything.

   It's _____.

7 The critics were right! It's a fabulous novel!

   It _____.

8 I tried and I tried but I really couldn't understand what was going on.

   I _____.

VOCABULARY: word sets

1 Write the words and phrases under the correct heading.

silent gleam lamp shriek silence straining ears candle strike a match whistle lantern cry flash audible echoes

Light	Sound

DICTATION

2a 1.29 Listen and write what you hear.

_____

_____

_____

_____

_____

_____

_____

2b Read what you have written and choose the best answer a, b or c.

1 This is a review of a ...

a) thriller.

b) science fiction or fantasy novel.

c) children's book.

2 The writer ...

a) likes the book.

b) isn't sure about the book.

c) doesn't like the book.

3 The story is told ...

a) by a wizard / magician.

b) by a little boy.

c) by someone else.

READING

3 Read the text. Match sentences A–F to gaps 1–6.

A He heard Sole talking to the soldier and then the echoes of footsteps as Sole and the soldier walked away.

B The soldier's shouts broke the silence and immediately four more of **them** rushed out between Peter and Sole.

C The gleam from **it** lit up the whole courtyard.

D He <u>was just falling asleep</u> when he heard a barely audible knock on his door.

It <u>was getting</u> late. Peter had long since given up waiting. ¹____ **He** quickly got up and opened the door. Sole <u>came rushing in, closed the door and put out</u> the lamp. 'Hurry,' he whispered. 'Soldiers
5 are looking for you. Be silent and follow **me**!' Sole opened the door again and looked out. After he <u>had checked</u> that the corridor was quiet and deserted, he led Peter out of the bedroom and down the stairs to the door of the courtyard. ²____ The small
10 light cast shadows across the walls. This frightened Peter even more. What was this all about? Why were soldiers looking for **him**?

'Listen to me, Peter,' Sole said. 'We don't have much time. We have to leave the castle quickly. Follow
15 me. We'll get some horses and we'll get out quickly.' Peter was going to ask why but Sole stopped him. 'Not now, Peter. We don't have time. Follow!' Sole slowly turned the door knob and opened **it**. He then stepped out into the courtyard. Peter followed him.

20 Suddenly, a cry was heard from the kitchens on the other side of the courtyard. The door of the kitchen burst open and out rushed a soldier carrying a lantern. ³____ Sole pushed Peter into a small corner, just out of the light. Peter couldn't see what was
25 happening. ⁴____ What should he do? Peter decided to wait. He would be safer here.

⁵____ It had to be Sole! He looked around and saw him waving from the gate. The gate was open and two horses were waiting for them. Peter jumped
30 out and ran across the courtyard but he hadn't seen the soldier who <u>had been standing</u> in front of the main hall. ⁶____ Peter was trapped. If Sole was ever going to show Peter some magic, now was the time!

E He'd been hiding in the corner for only five minutes when he heard a whistle.

F The corridor was still in darkness so Sole struck a match.

4 Read the text again. What do these words refer to?

1 He (line 2) _____

2 me (line 5) _____

3 him (line 12) _____

4 it (line 18) _____

5 it (option C) _____

6 them (option B) _____

GRAMMAR: narrative tenses, past perfect continuous

5 Match the underlined phrases from the text with the usage of the tenses.

1 An activity that was already in progress, and was interrupted by another action. (past continuous)

2 An ongoing action which happened before another action or time in the past. (past perfect continuous)

3 Events which took place one after another in a story and are seen as complete actions. (past simple)

4 Events which took place in the past, before another event in the past. (past perfect)

5 Events which set the scene and provide the background against which a story happens. (past continuous)

6 Read the sentences from the rest of the book. Write the incorrect verbs in the correct form.

dropped
1 Sole ~~had dropped~~ the sword and ran across the street.

2 Peter thought so hard he didn't see the man coming up behind him.

3 The ship had been finally moving. Peter could relax at last.

4 What had he doing when he first saw her?

5 The Chain went. Someone had taken it.

6 Peter stood up. He was waiting for this moment his whole life.

7 The glass was falling and smashed into a thousand pieces.

EVIL CHARACTERS

READING

1 Complete the text with the words in the box.

> tyrant   brutal   inflict   atrocities   sinister

Dear Students!

Welcome to the Creative Writing Course ELIT-305.
Let me make it clear that I am not a ¹_____.
I will expect you to work hard, but not too hard.

5 If you do not try, I will not ²_____ ³_____
punishment upon you, but you may fail the course
and then you will have to meet **me** again next
semester! I know that some of my ex-students
have accused me of committing ⁴_____

10 against humanity with the final exam but I assure
you I have no such ⁵_____ intention. **It**'s not
hard to pass this course. If you work, everything
will be fine. I do not want to terrify you and I will
not drink your blood. ☺

15 And here is your first task … what did you think
of the last paragraph? (i.e. Was **it** well-written?
What did you like about it? What didn't you like
about it?) Once you have answered **this**, prepare
an example of how you would have written the

20 paragraph.

Our next seminar will be called 'How great authors
wrote the best-known books.' We'll look at their
writing styles and see if we can learn anything
from **them**.

25 Dr Gregor Lloyd

2 Read the text and choose the best answer a, b or c.

1 This is an example of

a) a letter.

b) an introduction to a course.

c) a brochure.

2 If they fail the course, what will happen?

a) The students will have a meeting.

b) The students will do the course again.

c) The students will work harder.

3 What will happen in the next lesson?

a) The students will look at the writing habits of authors.

b) The students will write a paragraph.

c) Both.

3 What do these words refer to? Remember, *it* may refer to nothing.

1 me (line 7)   _____

2 It (line 11)   _____

3 it (line 16)   _____

4 this (line 18)   _____

5 them (line 24)   _____

LISTENING

4 **1.30** Listen to Dr Lloyd and match authors a–f with the writing habits 1–5. There is one author you don't need to use.

a) Ernest Hemingway   d) Proust

b) Anthony Trollope   e) Thomas Wolfe

c) Balzac   f) Somerset Maugham

1 needed to drink a lot of coffee

2 had to write a certain number of words every day

3 preferred to write in bed

4 started writing early in the morning

5 did all of his writing on his feet

Ernest Hemingway

Anthony Trollope

Proust

Thomas Wolfe

5 `1.30` **Listen again and decide whether these statements are true or false.**

1 Dr Lloyd thinks that Hemingway's habit is logical.

2 Writers are usually superstitious.

3 Trollope was a slow writer.

4 It is not a good idea to write in the mornings.

5 Many writers drink coffee to help them write.

6 Most writers' habits have a good reason.

7 Everyone knows the rules for writing.

8 Dr Lloyd will teach the students how to write.

GRAMMAR: *used to, would*

6 `1.30` **Listen again and write down the verb phrase with *used to* or *would* that Dr Lloyd uses with each author.**

1 Hemingway: <u>used to write</u>

2 Trollope: _____

3 Balzac: _____

4 Proust: _____

5 Wolfe: _____

7 Rewrite the sentences using *would* whenever possible, or *used to*.

1 Peter doesn't play tennis on Sundays any more.

_____

2 Simon works in Marketing. He's new.

_____

3 They aren't married any more.

_____

4 He has started talking to his brother again after ten years.

_____

5 The composer started his days with a swim.

_____

6 Is it true you went to school with Amanda?

_____

7 He has only been bad-tempered since he started this job last month.

_____

8 The children often sat by the river and watched the fish.

_____

9 Today people collect sweets at Halloween. This didn't happen when I was young.

_____

PRONUNCIATION: contrastive stress

8 `1.31` **Listen and underline the stressed word in these sentences.**

1 Bart is living in Japan.

2 Bart used to live in Japan.

LISTEN BETTER

When a speaker is correcting another speaker, the stress will fall on the part of the sentence that the speaker is correcting. So, in Exercise 8, the second speaker is responding to somebody who said *Bart lives in Japan*.

9a `1.32` **Listen and tick the sentences where the speaker is correcting someone else.**

1 Sarah used to walk to school.

2 My boss used to write for a newspaper.

3 The school used to offer scholarships.

4 His team used to be good.

5 Eagles used to be common in these hills.

9b Practise saying the sentences.

READING

1 Read the text and correct these sentences.

1 Many well-known writers are now using Keitai.

_____

2 Keitai novels can only be seen on your phone.

_____

3 Keitai novels are mostly written for children.

_____

4 The most popular Keitai novels are thrillers.

_____

5 Critics have been very positive about Keitai.

_____

6 Anyone can now write novels at home.

_____

Mobile phone novelists are hitting the bestseller lists as a new generation of writers are creating novels on the keys of their telephones. In Japan, where most technological trends start, keitai shosetsu (literally 'portable (phone) novel') are a publishing phenomenon. Of the top ten bestselling fiction works in Japan in the first half of 2007, five started as Keitai novels.

Keitai novels are usually written by first-time writers and are quite basic in style and content. Yet that doesn't stop them from joining the paper publishing world. One Keitai novel, *Love Sky*, has now been turned into a real book, has sold more than 1.3 million copies and is being made into a film.

The success of Keitai relies on an audience of people who regularly use mobile phones for messaging and phoning. In Japan this means girls and young women in their twenties. It is no surprise that it is dramas and love stories that are the most successful.

There has been a lot of criticism of Keitai novels by writers and other members of the world of literature but the fact remains that Keitai gives everyone the chance to write novels, wherever they are.

KEY LANGUAGE: proposing, bargaining, talking about needs/ expectations

2a Match the sentences halves.

1 In this case,

2 We feel that if you agreed with us on the deal,

3 You'll find it's

4 Really, we weren't expecting

5 If you included the other program we talked about,

6 How about if I talked to our development team

7 I'd like to make

8 Why don't you

9 We need time to think about this,

10 Could I suggest

a) to pay as much as that.

b) and take some advice.

c) we think 25 percent is more appropriate.

d) show the product to your investors?

e) a proposal.

f) we meet again next week?

g) very good value for money.

h) and got back to you on that?

i) you'd be guaranteed to make a huge profit.

j) it'd make it more attractive for us.

2b [1.33] **Listen to a meeting to discuss a business deal and check your answers.**

1 Underline the adverbs of degree in the box.

extremely	complete	quickly	almost
really	absolutely	prettily	friendly
very	incredibly	pretty	

WRITING SKILLS: a blog

2 Add the adverbs from Exercise 1 to the blog of the writer Jake Arnold. Use each one no more than once.

DAY 13 OF THE NEW NOVEL

Hi everyone! I still haven't decided on the title for the book. People think choosing a title is ¹_____ easy but in fact it's ²_____ difficult. I've tried six different titles already! If someone could possibly suggest a title, I would be very grateful.

This morning I finished Chapter 2. It's already getting ³_____ frightening … but not too frightening I hope! I can't decide why the ghost only lives on the top floor. The book works better if the hero has a safe place in the house, like the ground floor.

Again, I haven't decided on the name of the hero. I know he's in his thirties, in fact he's ⁴_____ forty. We also know he has just bought the house and is ⁵_____ happy with it. Of course he doesn't know about the ghost yet!

The publishing house has changed the deadline again! I have been asked if it would be possible to submit the draft by the end of December. Well, that's ⁶_____ impossible! There's no chance I can make that date. It would mean that I would have to write a chapter a day. I am afraid I will not be able to write that much.

Anyway, I need to get back to work if I can meet the deadline. I'm going to be ⁷_____ busy for the next few days so sorry if I don't have time to tell you what's been happening.

3 Underline three sentences in the text which are written in the wrong style for a blog. Which style are they in?

_____

4 Here are the notes for Jake Arnold's next blog entry. Write the blog, using the notes.

Sorry / not written / busy. Good news!
Decide / title / 'Madwoman in Attic' / What think? / now / ghost / not top floor but attic / hero / hear / footsteps / above him / goes to attic / sees young girl / don't know / happen next / tell you next blog.
Finished Chapter 5 / Hero name / Peter Youngblood / is architect / so understands / houses built / need someone / knows about the ghost / maybe the person who sold the house / too easy? / what you think?
Publishers / happy / Chapters 1 and 2 / deadline now February / Am lot happier.

_____

_____

_____

_____

_____

_____

_____

_____

7 Architecture

7.1 MY FAVOURITE BUILDING

VOCABULARY: describing buildings

1 Fill the gaps with one word. The first letter(s) are given to help you.

1 The house isn't just old. It's a_____ – it was built in about 1200.

2 The house is really di_____. There's water dripping through the roof.

3 His company takes old, very r_____ houses and turns them into perfect places to live.

4 The design of the ceiling in the entrance is an example of the c_____ French style.

5 It's such an e_____ house. You would think the president lived there.

6 When the designs for the building were first shown, we all thought it was so new and in_____.

7 The building design is a little out of date. I would have preferred a more co_____ style.

8 The castle looks m_____ against the background of the mountains, especially in the evenings.

9 The de_____ building across the road used to be a school.

10 The windows in their new house are really u_____. It's a pity they can't change them.

2 Read the report and put the underlined words in the correct place.

> The decisions of the Rother Planning Committee are as follows.
>
> 1 To <u>construct</u> a plan for a new primary school in Peasmarsh, from Tel Co. They should <u>rebuild</u> the building according to Government Specification L242.
>
> 2 To <u>design</u> the Community Centre in Northiam and, in its place, <u>demolish</u> an Unemployment Office.
>
> 3 To <u>maintain</u> Leasam House. It's now been derelict for five years and needs work.
>
> 4 To ask the government for extra money to <u>restore</u> the current bus service to Icklesham.
>
> 5 To replace the furniture that was <u>commission</u> in the fire at the Council Offices in Rye
>
> 6 To <u>damaged</u> the ticket office outside the bus station at Camber Sands that was destroyed in last year's storm.

TRANSLATION

3 Translate these words into your own language. Can they be used to describe things other than buildings?

1 impressive _____   4 traditional _____

2 stylish _____   5 imposing _____

3 graceful _____   6 ornate _____

GRAMMAR: the passive (1)

1 Write these active sentences in the passive.

1 I will tell Alessandra of the developments after the meeting.

_____

2 The builders are renovating the offices at the moment.

_____

3 We will maintain the facility until the end of the year.

_____

4 We restore about six houses every year.

_____

5 The council is commissioning a new bus station.

_____

6 The theatre group won't pay for the damage to the stage.

_____

7 The committee has made its decision and will not change it.

_____

8 People drink more cola than fruit juice every day.

_____

9 I want someone to drive me to work.

_____

10 I don't like people talking to me.

_____

2a Underline the phrases that can be omitted from these sentences. Sometimes nothing can be omitted.

1 I'm being sent on a course by my company.

2 The cards were sent out yesterday by people who wanted them to arrive on time.

3 It was made by the Schengen company.

4 The prisoner was taken by police to the new prison outside town.

5 The wall was damaged by something last night.

6 The car was thoroughly tested by the end of the week.

2b Tick the correct reason for omitting the phrases above.

a) The subject of the sentence is not important or not known.

b) The agent is not important or not known.

c) There should be no object.

d) There should be no information after the verb.

DICTATION

3 2.2 Listen and write what you hear.

Theme hotels with a difference

_____

_____

_____

_____

_____

_____

_____

_____

_____

_____

4 Read what you have written and choose the correct answer a, b or c.

1 If you try to do something different, you can

a) improve your position in the market.

b) lose your position in the market.

c) hold your position in the market.

2 How many tourists are looking for hotels with a difference?

a) very few

b) some

c) many

3 These Theme Hotels can help you

a) have new ideas.

b) make more money.

c) change your style.

READING

5 Read the rest of the text about theme hotels and match headings A–D with paragraphs 1–3. There is one heading you don't need to use.

A For those who are not afraid of heights.

B For those who prefer under to over.

C For those who like the smell of danger.

D For those who need cooling down.

6 Underline examples of the present simple passive, future passive and present continuous passive in the text.

READ BETTER

Scanning is the ability to find key information in a large text. When scanning, you should remember the following things:

a Don't read the whole text word by word.

b Read the questions.

c Quickly skim the text looking for the key words or similar ideas.

d Underline the key words.

e Read only the sections that contain the key words or similar ideas.

7 According to the text, which hotel (or hotels) …

1 is better than it actually looks from outside?

2 allows you to live in a similar way to the people who live there?

3 gives a choice of different types of rooms?

4 changes at different times of the year?

5 is preferred by the writer?

1

Personally, I like sunny beaches and lots of sand and blue sea but the Icehotel is exactly what it says it is – a hotel made out of ice. Opened in 1990, 30,000 tons of snow and 10,000 tons of crystal clear ice are used every year to keep the happy hotel guests freezing cold. Admittedly, a choice of conventional rooms is also offered so there is no reason why you need to freeze in your own room. In addition, the hotel offers other great events such as safari trips out onto the ice on snowmobiles, fabulous examples of ice art and there is a church made entirely out of ice. Unfortunately the ice part of the hotel is closed in the summer – it doesn't exist then! The hotel is really good value for money, but only if you like being cold.

2

Over the last twenty or thirty years the African tourist industry has started living up to its potential, and Ngong House is now being promoted as the number one hotel throughout the continent. At first glance, however, you might want to think again. There is no hotel, really. There is a collection of tree houses, and from outside these houses made of local wood do not look very inviting. The reality though is that inside the rooms are really elegant and the visitor is treated to a holiday of luxury. The location is also magnificent and it is an experience of a lifetime to see the sunset over the Ngong Hills. You are also within an hour's drive of two of the best safari parks in the world. All this and more for £150 a night.

3

The town of Coober Pedy in Australia is famous for its opal, the valuable white stone that is mined here. As it is so hot in this part of the world, it is no surprise that many people live underground. So, it's not so strange to find that there is an underground hotel there too – the Desert Cave hotel. The visitor is given the choice of staying underground or above ground but this really is no choice at all as the only really special thing about Coober Pedy (apart from the opal) is the opportunity to stay underground. The visitors' book is full of people saying they had a beautiful sleep in these underground rooms and I have to agree with them. It's also not just the rooms that are underground. There are shops, a café, an interactive centre about opal, which is being renovated at the moment, and a games room. All underground. You have to ask yourself if there is any reason to go above ground. And that's the problem. Unless you are interested in opal, there really isn't much else to do above ground. The brochure states that more activities will be introduced in the next year but until then, it's a long way to go to get a good night's sleep.

VOCABULARY:
idioms, prefixes

1 Fill the gaps to complete the idioms.

1 What I've done will not let things go back to the way they were. =
I've _____ bridges.

2 We'll think about it when it happens. =
_____ bridge when we come to it.

3 It's happened now and there's nothing we can do about it. =
That's _____ bridge.

4 I need to resolve the argument I had with my best friend. =
I _____ bridges.

2 Complete the sentences with the correct form of a word from the box.

vitalise	placed	crowded	come	usual
sensitive	define	important	understand	
~~disputable~~	soluble			

1 No one can argue about it. The facts are
indisputable .

2 Everyone says the programme is boring. We need to _____ it.

3 I'm sorry, I _____ you. I thought you said you didn't want to come.

4 Where's my book? I seem to have _____ it.

5 I've never seen that before. It's very _____, isn't it?

6 Could you please _____ that word? Its meaning won't be clear to everybody.

7 How could you tell him he was fat? That was really _____.

8 We can't let you in. It's already _____ inside.

READING

3 Read the text and answer the questions.

1 Which site wasn't built by Poles? _____

2 Which site is a copy of the original? _____

3 Which is the latest project? _____

4 Which was the biggest building site in Europe in the 1900s? _____

In the nineteen nineties, Warsaw was called the second largest building site in Europe after Berlin. In fact, the rebuilding of Warsaw had started much earlier, in 1945 in fact.

Warsaw has now been transformed into a modern city. The interesting thing, however, is that Warsaw has also looked backwards to rebuild the great buildings of the past and make sure its history has not been forgotten. Some of the highlights of this are:

The Old Town

Ninety percent of the Old Town was destroyed in 1944. However between 1949 and 1963 it was completely rebuilt.

The Palace of Science and Culture

Up until the arrival of the American-style skyscraper, this was the tallest building in Poland. Built on the orders of Stalin between 1952 and 1955, it was built entirely by Russian workers.

The Warsaw Uprising Monuments

The first of these beautiful monuments was presented in 1989. They are intended to help people remember an event that until recently has largely been forgotten by the outside world.

New World (Nowy Swiat) Street

The cultural shopping centre of Warsaw. Since 1996 the street has been completely renovated as a modern shopping street which still retains a taste of the past.

The Little Insurgent

LISTENING

4 `2.3` **Listen to four people talking about sites in Warsaw. Tick the sites they like and cross the sites they dislike.**

	A	B	C	D
New World Street				
Palace of Science and Culture				
The Old Town				
Warsaw Uprising Monuments				

GRAMMAR: the passive (2)

5a `2.3` **Listen again and fill the gaps.**

1 ... like a picture _____ as soldiers _____ underground to escape from the guns.

2 People forget that the Old Town _____ recently.

3 When it _____, most Polish people took no notice of it.

4 I know it _____ a bad name by people ...

5 Think about all the buildings that _____ and rebuilt at that time, and yet it remained.

6 A whole area _____ and then rebuilt in less than twenty years.

7 I _____ that it's not really Polish but that doesn't matter.

8 Warsaw _____ in a way that brings the past and the future together.

5b **Which past passive forms did you use? Label the extracts above a, b or c.**

a) *has/have + been* + past participle – present perfect passive

b) *was/were + being* + past participle – past continuous passive

c) *was/were* + past participle – past simple passive

6 **Add one word to each sentence to make it passive.**

                         been
1 I don't think the minister has ⋏ understood.

2 David saw that the school still being built.

3 The trip had made a hundred times.

4 He seen outside the building at eight.

5 The gardens designed in 1821.

6 At midnight the votes were still counted and no one knew the result.

The Palace of Science and Culture in Warsaw

7 **What is wrong with these sentences and why?**

1 The tallest, ugliest and most unpopular building in Warsaw, The Palace of Science and Culture has been attracting attention recently.

_____

2 Warsaw University was opened in 1816. It is known to be very popular with students.

_____

8 **Correct these sentence with the passive infinitive.**

1 I want to see in my new dress.

_____

2 The book is expect to finish by the end of the month.

_____

3 The school is build next month.

_____

4 Children are give new classes next year.

_____

LISTENING

1 `2.4` **Listen to the discussion and choose the best answer a, b or c.**

1 Who is talking?

   a) two students

   b) two lecturers

   c) two administrators

2 What are they talking about?

   a) the next lesson

   b) university courses

   c) an old teacher

3 What's their biggest problem?

   a) what happens in the first year

   b) the bookshop

   c) a visiting professor

KEY LANGUAGE: talking about requirements

2 `2.4` **Listen again and put the phrases in order (1–8).**

a) We should also offer … ____

b) We'd have to find out … ____

c) It's vital … ____

d) It's absolutely essential … ____

e) We've got to … ____

f) We need to … ____

g) We certainly need … ____

h) It might be a good idea … ____

3a **Put the words in the correct order to make sentences.**

1 a should gift also we free offer

   _____

2 trains if have to are we'd running out find the

   _____

3 March building the finished vital have by we it's

   _____

4 soon as essential see as possible him to it's absolutely

   _____

5 time party got we've change the of the to

   _____

6 shopping need we go weekend certainly to this

   _____

7 think through we need carefully to this

   _____

8 him give idea a might call to be it good a

   _____

3b `2.5` **Listen and check your answers.**

PRONUNCIATION: emphasis

4a `2.6` **Listen and underline the stressed words.**

1 It's absolutely essential to cancel the loan.

2 You need to consider the consequences of your actions!

3 It might be a good idea if you told him.

4 It's vital we have him give the news as soon as possible.

4b **Why are the words stressed?**

a) to emphasise who is doing it

b) to emphasise what needs/should be done

c) to emphasise how desirable/essential/possible something is

WRITING SKILLS:
a description of a building

1 Read the notes for an essay on the Dolmabahçe Palace in Istanbul. Put the paragraphs in the correct order using the topic sentences to help you.

1 ___ 2 ___ 3 ___ 4 ___

A:
TOPIC SENTENCE: The palace cost the equivalent of 35 tons of gold to build.
SUPPORTING IDEAS:
   14 tons of gold for interior ceiling
   most expensive ceiling in the world, possibly

B:
TOPIC SENTENCE: In my opinion, although Dolmabahçe is much smaller than Versailles, it is a fantastic piece of work by Garabet Balyan.
SUPPORTING IDEAS:
   father told go and see great example of extreme ornamentation
   understood why father called Dolmabahçe second Versailles

C:
TOPIC SENTENCE: As well as the ceiling, another attraction is the world's largest Bohemian crystal chandelier.
SUPPORTING IDEAS:
   750 lamps
   weighs 4.5 tons
   largest collection of Bohemian and Baccarat chandeliers in the world
   Sultan sent men travelling empire to find most beautiful

D:
TOPIC SENTENCE: The Dolmabahçe Palace in Istanbul is the best example of late Ottoman architecture.
SUPPORTING IDEAS:
   leading architect was Garabet Balyan
   commissioned by Sultan to complete
   advised to make as beautiful as Versailles
   Ottoman Empire period of decline
   1850s – one of weakest Empires in Europe
   Sultan provided anything needed
   completed in nine years

WRITE BETTER

When we write notes we divide each paragraph into two sections:
TOPIC SENTENCE – This is usually the first sentence of the paragraph that tells you the topic of that paragraph.
SUPPORTING IDEAS – This is a list of all the important information you wish to include, in note form.

2 Read the extracts from the essay. Rewrite the underlined sections, replacing the words in italics to avoid repetition.

1 … just to cover the interior ceiling of the palace, <u>making *the ceiling* possibly the most</u> …

_____

2 My father told me to go and see this great example of extreme ornamentation <u>and once I *had gone and seen this great example of extreme ornamentation*</u>, …

_____

3 … Bohemian and Baccarat crystal chandeliers in the world. <u>To achieve *having the largest collection of Bohemian and Baccarat chandeliers*</u> …

_____

4 Garabet Balyan was commissioned by the Sultan to complete the palace. <u>*Garabet Balyan* was advised to make *the Dolmabahçe Palace* as beautiful as Versailles.</u>

_____

5 The architect needed to get the Domabahçe Palace completed and <u>*the architect* was able to *complete the Dolmabahçe Palace* in nine years.</u>

_____

3 Use the notes in Exercise 1 and the corrected extracts in Exercise 2 to write the essay.

_____
_____
_____
_____
_____
_____
_____
_____
_____
_____

8 Globalisation

8.1 GLOBALISATION – GOOD OR BAD?

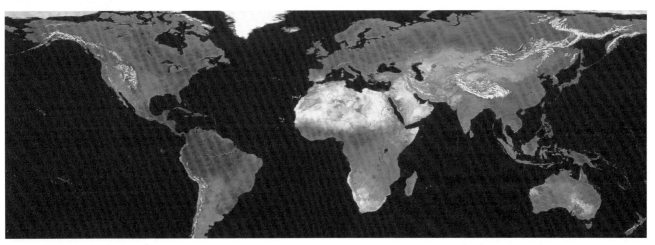

VOCABULARY: word combinations

1a Match 1–10 with a–j.

1	consumer	a)	companies
2	natural	b)	change
3	climate	c)	resources
4	global	d)	choice
5	corporate	e)	markets
6	multinational	f)	greed
7	fair	g)	warming
8	child	h)	rights
9	human	i)	labour
10	free	j)	trade

1b Complete the sentences with word combinations from above.

1 I only drink _____ coffee. This is coffee that is bought directly from poor coffee growers.

2 The death of the dinosaurs is usually blamed on a major _____, with the beginning of the Ice Age.

3 Local companies and industries cannot hope to compete with _____.

4 _____ results in lower educational standards of future generations as children don't have time to go to school.

5 Overpopulation indirectly results in the overuse of _____. Therefore, we need to think of alternative sources of power.

6 The hot summer and lack of water this year have convinced me that we are experiencing _____.

7 There is no _____ here. Either you buy it at the supermarket or you don't buy it at all.

8 Having _____ may mean less tax for the government but will encourage more trade.

PRONUNCIATION

2 [2.7] Listen to the word combinations. Does the main stress appear on the first or second word? Which word is different to all the others?

1	*second*	6	_____
2	_____	7	_____
3	_____	8	_____
4	_____	9	_____
5	_____	10	_____

TRANSLATION

3 Translate the word combinations into your language.

1	_____	6	_____
2	_____	7	_____
3	_____	8	_____
4	_____	9	_____
5	_____	10	_____

DICTATION

1 [2.8] Listen and write what you hear.

_____

_____

_____

_____

_____

_____

_____

VOCABULARY: abstract nouns

2a Underline the five abstract nouns mentioned in the dictation.

2b Match the abstract nouns to these comments.

1 We need a lot of this if we are going to come up with some new ideas. _____

2 How can I complain if I don't know who my manager is? _____

3 The best thing to do is get to know as many people as you can at the party. _____

4 Sales and Marketing are working together on this project. _____

5 I was going to sign up for Art but John suggested that History was better. _____

EXTRA VOCABULARY: more abstract nouns

3 Tick the correct description of an abstract noun.

a) A noun that describes an action that you or someone else can do.

b) A noun that describes an object or a thing that you can see, hear or feel.

c) A noun that describes something you cannot sense.

4 Underline the abstract nouns. Circle any noun that can be abstract or concrete.

automobile	market	coin	joy
responsibility	argument	earthquake	
supervision	meeting	love	

READING

5 Read the text. Match the information 1–6 with paragraphs A–E.

1 Zuckerberg doesn't live life like a millionaire. ____

2 His school didn't like his original project. ____

3 It is a risk for Zuckerberg to keep the company. ____

4 Zuckerberg wants to hold on to his company. ____

5 Facebook is expected to keep growing. ____

6 Zuckerberg started Facebook at school. ____/____

A Mark Zuckerberg's life so far is like a movie script. A supersmart kid invents a tech phenomenon while attending college. Just three years later, what started as a networking site for college students has managed to become a tool for 19 million registered users. More than half of the users visit every day. It is now the sixth most visited site in the United States. It also rates as the number one photo-sharing site on the Web, with 6 million pictures uploaded daily. A recent report projected that Facebook would generate $969 million in revenue, with 48 million users, by 2010.

B However, on meeting Zuckerberg you find it easy to stop thinking of him as the head of a world-beating organisation. He still lives in a rented apartment, with a mattress on the floor and only two chairs and a table for furniture. He walks or bikes to the office every day.

C Zuckerberg doesn't deny starting life as a computer hacker. One night early in his second year, he hacked into Harvard's student records. He then opened a basic site called Facemash, which paired photos of undergraduates and invited visitors to determine which one was 'hotter'. Four hours, 450 visitors, and 22,000 photo views later, Harvard closed Zuckerberg's Internet connection. Within a short time, he had set up the Facebook template and let students fill in their own information. Thefacebook.com, as it was originally called, launched on 4 February, 2004. Within two weeks, half the Harvard student body had signed up. Before

long, it was up to two-thirds. In November 2004, Facebook passed the one million users mark. By the autumn of 2005, there were five million users who visited the site at least once a month.

D Facebook's staggering success has resulted in quite a few concerned organisations trying to buy out the owners of Facebook. For example, it was reported that Yahoo had made a $1 billion offer to buy Facebook. Zuckerberg and his partners politely told them to look elsewhere. They didn't even need time to stop and think. When asked, Zuckerberg seems uninterested in selling. 'I'm here to build something for the long term,' he says. 'Anything else is a distraction.' He and his colleagues are true believers.

E However, hanging over the Facebook talk is the ghost of Friendster, the first significant social-networking site. It reportedly turned down a chance to sell out to Google in 2002 for $30 million, approximately worth about $1 billion today. Now Friendster is struggling, trying to stay with the next generation of sites. The same thing could happen to Facebook.

6 Read the text again. Are these statements true or false, according to the text?

1 Facebook is the most popular site for sharing pictures.

2 Mark Zuckerberg behaves like the owner of a major organisation.

3 The original Facebook was only for students at his university.

4 Zuckerberg illegally used university records.

5 In less than a year there were five million users visiting the site.

6 Zuckerberg thought carefully about selling Facebook.

7 The story of another website shows that Zuckerberg is probably making the right decision.

GRAMMAR: verb patterns

7 Write the verbs under the correct heading.

manage	stop	deny	tell	persuade
suggest	forget	try	enjoy	seem
encourage	want	remind	finish
promise	need

verb + inf	verb + -*ing*	verb + obj + inf	verb + -*ing* or inf

8 Tick the correct sentences. Correct the incorrect verb patterns.

to lock
1 Peter always forgets ~~locking~~ the door at night.

2 I think you should invite to come him.

3 I want to see if they have any copies left.

4 They attempted seeing him but it was impossible.

5 Do you remember walking through the park last week?

6 I am trying to practise playing the piano more.

7 Would you consider to leave early?

8 I've been trying making the TV work all night.

VOCABULARY: the media

1 Complete the text with the words in the box.

| paparazzi celebrity characters coverage newspapers press programme televised broadcast |

Most of the time, when people think of role models, they think of people who have
¹_____ status, or ²_____
from TV series. Maybe these are the people that the
³_____ spend all their time chasing.
Certainly the ⁴_____ gives a lot of
⁵_____ to these people because it sells
their ⁶_____. However, this doesn't
make these people role models. Role models can
come from any walk of life. For example, you can
find business role models. At the moment there is a
⁷_____ that is being
⁸_____ on BBC called 'The Apprentice'.
This is a competition to find the future super
businessman or woman. The presenter, who is also
a very successful businessman, is presented as
a role model for others. The programme is
⁹_____ every Tuesday. Don't miss it.

2 Correct the media expressions.

1 Right now, Casper is at the point of his career.

2 If you go out the back way, you won't get dropped by fans.

3 The paparazzi make sure that I'm always in the brightlights.

4 At her wedding, she was the centre of attendance.

LISTENING

3 ⏸ 2.9 Listen and tick the picture which best shows the situation in the listening. What helped you decide?

LISTEN BETTER

Exercise 3 is an example of inference. When we infer from a text (listening or reading), we understand something, even though we don't actually read it or hear it. We can use inference to understand general points, draw conclusions or understand meaning from context.

4 Use inference to answer these questions.

1 'The smoke was so thick we couldn't see anything. We had to wait until it dissipated.'

dissipated means:

a) became thicker

b) became thinner

c) became difficult to breathe

2 'Helen wiped her tears away and tried to smile.'

Helen was:

a) tired

b) happy

c) sad

3 'The decision was made. We put on our masks and picked up our guns.'

What decision was made?

a) to visit a friend

b) to rob a bank

c) to go hunting

5 `2.9` **Listen again and choose the correct answer a, b, c or d.**

1 What does Mike do on an average day?

  a) prepares posters and other types of promotion

  b) meets and talks to people

  c) relaxes in his office

  d) runs a delivery service

2 What does Dr Spencer think of Mike?

  a) He is trying to do the right thing.

  b) He is a role model.

  c) He is not very good at what he does.

  d) He should answer some questions.

3 What does *outsourcing* mean?

  a) meeting lots of people and keeping them happy

  b) contracting jobs to other companies

  c) doing everything in the company

  d) trying to work on many contracts at the same time

GRAMMAR:
have something done

6a **Read these extracts from the listening. Tick examples of *have something done*.**

1 I discovered early on in this business that you have to look after the customer.

2 Sorry, we've had to move the date of printing.

3 So, we had the designs prepared by a design company.

4 Well I'm not sure you can have a role model for business.

5 Sorry, but we've had the wrong posters delivered.

6 Every Monday we have all our stuff collected by a delivery service.

7 It does have to be done for a good reason.

8 We had everything boxed by a packaging company.

9 What we do is we meet people who want to have their product advertised.

10 I've never had a call from a customer saying that they've had their campaign ruined by our poor posters or brochures.

6b **Match uses a–c with the extracts you ticked. Some extracts can match more than one use.**

a) When an action is done for us by somebody else.

  Extracts: _____

b) Something that happens to us which we have little or no control over.

  Extracts: _____

c) Unexpected or unpleasant things that happen to us.

  Extracts: _____

7a **Rewrite these sentences using the form *have something done*.**

1 Our windows are cleaned once a month.

  _____

2 Surprisingly, the books were sent to us two weeks earlier than planned.

  _____

3 Have you got someone to finish the report?

  _____

4 The dentist hasn't checked my teeth for over a year.

  _____

5 A ghostwriter is writing my autobiography.

  _____

6 The government checks our school every six months.

  _____

7 Someone has stolen my car!

  _____

7b `2.10` **Listen and check your answers. Then practise saying the sentences yourself.**

KEY LANGUAGE: clarifying

1a Correct these phrases that we use for clarification.

1 What ~~^~~ *do* you mean ~~of~~ *by* that?
2 Or to do it another route …
3 Basically that I'm saying that …
4 Could you give a special example?
5 Which I really wanted to was …
6 Sorry, I am not knowing what you mean.
7 To be more present, we really …
8 Could you do more specify?
9 Could you explore that in more part?
10 Let rephrase me that.

1b Complete the dialogue with some of the phrases above.

A: I think it's all about personality.
B: 1________________
A: OK. 2________________ it is the personality of a person that is mainly responsible for role modelling.
B: 3________________
A: Don't you? Hmm. 4________________ then. To become a role model you need to have a certain type of personality.
B: 5________________
A: Of course. Think about a pop star. What sort of personality do they need? Well, they have to be ambitious and they have to be outgoing to begin with. 6________________ is that if you haven't got the right personality, you're unlikely to be a role model. A quiet, shy person is not a role model for a pop star.

1c 2.11 Listen and check your answers.

STUDY SKILLS: summarising

1 Read the essay on businessman Alan Sugar. Underline the topic sentences and important ideas.

In this paper I would like to discuss the question 'Is Alan Sugar a role model for people going into business?' There are certainly reasons to answer 'yes' or 'no' to this question.

Alan Sugar has definitely been a successful businessman and celebrity. He left school at 16 with no qualifications and started his own business selling electrical goods out of the back of a van. He now has an estimated fortune of £830 million and is the 84th richest man in the UK. His Amstrad CPC 464 was one of the first home computers and by the end of the 1980s Amstrad had a stock market value of £1.25 billion. In the nineties and later he started buying and selling companies such as Sinclair, Betacom, Viglen and eventually sold Amstrad itself, at a profit. He was also Chairman of Tottenham Hotspur Football Club. He has now become a TV celebrity with his own TV series 'The Apprentice', which is a reality TV show where a group of young business people try to win an important position in Alan Sugar's company.

On the other hand, Alan Sugar has, for a long time, not been very popular with many people. He has a reputation for being a ruthless and insensitive man. He has treated the contestants on 'The Apprentice' badly. In fact Alan Sugar is best known for saying 'You're fired!' to someone in every episode. Many businesspeople have also said that 'The Apprentice' actually shows you how not to run a business, rather than how to run one. Even his business skills have been questioned. Amstrad was very unsuccessful in the nineties and many people blame Sugar personally for that failure.

In conclusion, Alan Sugar is certainly not an ideal role model. However, in my opinion Alan Sugar is a role model because he started with nothing and finished a millionaire. Such a story surely has lessons for all of us.

2 You have been asked to write a summary of the essay, using no more than 130 words. Which of these sentences should you use to write your summary? Use your answers to Exercise 1 to help you.

a) There are good reasons for and against.

b) Alan Sugar has been a successful businessman.

c) He left school at sixteen.

d) He sold electrical goods from the back of a van.

e) He has a fortune of £830 million and is the 84th richest man.

f) He owned Amstrad.

g) Amstrad was one of the first companies to make home computers.

h) By the end of the eighties Amstrad had a stock market share of £1.25 billion.

i) In the nineties he bought and sold companies at a profit.

j) Examples were Sinclair, Betacom, Viglen and Amstrad.

k) He was Chairman of a football club and now has a successful TV series.

l) It's a reality TV show for young businesspeople.

m) On the other hand, Alan Sugar is not popular with many people.

n) People say he is ruthless and insensitive.

o) He treats his contestants badly on 'The Apprentice'.

p) 'The Apprentice' does not show an example of how to run a business.

q) His business skills have been questioned.

r) Even Sugar admitted Amstrad could've done better if he had made the right decisions.

s) The writer thinks he is a role model because he started with nothing and then became rich.

t) There are lessons for all of us in his life.

WRITING SKILLS: a summary

3 Shorten these extracts from paragraphs 2 and 3 of the text, using the way suggested in brackets.

1 He left school at 16 with no qualifications and started his own business selling electrical goods out of the back of a van. (joining clauses)

_____

_____

2 In the nineties and later he started buying and selling companies such as Sinclair, Betacom, Viglen and eventually sold Amstrad itself, at a profit. (removing examples)

_____

_____

3 He has now become a TV celebrity with his own TV series 'The Apprentice', which is a reality TV show where a group of young business people try to win an important position in Alan Sugar's company. (joining clauses)

_____

_____

4 Write a summary of paragraph 3 using ellipsis and any other techniques that will help. Use no more than 40 words.

_____

_____

_____

_____

_____

_____

_____

9 Art

9.1 WHAT IS ART?

VOCABULARY: art and artists

1 Fill the gaps in the text with one word. The first two letters are given to help you.

There are three exhibitions I suggest you get down to visit this week. The first is a ¹ pr_____ at Huston's, so get to see it before everyone else does! These are Anotoly Ribienko's latest works and there are some marvellous examples here of some ² gr_____ techniques that he has been trying out. The collection includes his ³ ma_____ 'Matka'. Ribienko is one of the most exciting ⁴ pa_____ around and his work with oils is particularly popular with ⁵ co_____, who will pay hundred of thousands of pounds for his works.

The second exhibition is a ⁶ re_____ of the art of the ⁷ sc_____ Selma Howard. Selma was always ⁸ co_____ with her concrete handbags and paper mobile phones, but her later political work was very ⁹ th_____. People forget that she also did some very interesting traditional statues. She is a great loss to the art world.

The final exhibition shows a collection of famous paintings of the Renaissance period. All ¹⁰ ar_____ will enjoy it but it is the sort of exhibition that ¹¹ cr_____ like to complain about, saying it is popularising art. Still, I think it's worth a visit.

2 Match the style of art or art movement with the correct meaning.

1 contemporary

2 realism

3 modern

4 abstract

a) shows or describes things, especially unpleasant things, as they really are in life

b) consists of shapes and patterns that do not look like real people or things

c) belongs to the present time

d) uses styles that have been recently developed and are very different from traditional styles

TRANSLATION

3 Translate the words in Exercise 2 into your language.

1 _____

2 _____

3 _____

4 _____

VOCABULARY: words from the lesson

4 Delete the extra word in the following expressions.

1 I'm not really good into that sort of thing.

2 I'd really be recommend it.

3 It was the one of the best shows I have ever seen.

4 It wasn't worth to the effort.

5 It didn't really live it up to my expectations.

6 The critic said it wasn't very good time.

7 I was really moved in by it.

READING

1 **Read the message and answer the questions.**

1 What do we know about Cassandra?

  a) She is an experienced amateur photographer.

  b) She is a professional photographer.

  c) She has never done a photoshoot before.

2 Where is she planning to do the photoshoot?

  a) on a hill

  b) in an empty house

  c) in a family house

3 What is Cassandra looking for?

  a) equipment

  b) advice from a real photographer

  c) someone to help on the photoshoot

Photoshoot planning

***posted by Cassandra Morley, Feb 15, 2007;
12:39 p.m.***

Hi! I'm a student planning my first photoshoot for a project. I'm a little worried as I'm not sure what I need to think about. I want to be sure that it all runs smoothly and would love to know what sort of things I need to plan for.

The location for the photoshoot is a derelict house on the side of a hill in the Lake District (see attached). Behind the house the hill is all stone and the image of the house against the side of this stone wall has real potential for a deeply moving picture.

As I said, this will be the first time that I have worked on a full photoshoot although I have some experience of working with photographs and pictures and, of course, I've taken holiday photographs. I'm afraid I'll be utterly useless without some help.

I'm going up there on Tuesday so I would really appreciate some advice from a highly qualified photographer.

Thanks in advance,

Cassandra

VOCABULARY:
common adverb/adjective collocations

2 **Underline three examples of collocations in the text.**

3 **Complete the sentences by adding an adjective to the adverb to make collocations.**

1 His arrival in London was entirely _____.

2 He won't talk to you. He's painfully

  _____.

3 The criticism by the judge on the poor boy was totally _____. He didn't do anything wrong.

4 The actions of the Conservation Group have been heavily _____ in their report and must result in changes.

5 Our holiday experience on the Orkney Islands was totally _____! I never expected it would be so good.

6 A highly _____ researcher is needed to lead the team on the project.

7 How can he say that the water levels have increased in the last three months? It's completely

  _____.

8 The film on the Bosnian War was deeply

  _____.

PRONUNCIATION

4a **Write the number of syllables then underline the main stress in each phrase.**

1 highly praised ___

2 totally unbelievable ___

3 utterly different ___

4 utterly impossible ___

4b [2.12] **Listen and check your answers.**

LISTENING

LISTEN BETTER

When listening for specific information, make sure you know what to listen for. If there are questions, read the questions carefully and underline the key words. Then, for every key word make a list of words with similar meaning that may be used in the listening. Listen for the key words or synonyms and you will find your answer.

5 **2.13** Listen to Cassandra's phone call with a photographer. Tick the topics that are discussed.

1 getting people to help ☐
2 making a list of things you need ☐
3 bringing food ☐
4 checking the weather ☐
5 taking warm clothes ☐
6 bringing lights ☐
7 painting ☐
8 checking the house ☐
9 having the right camera ☐
10 controlling the environment ☐
11 taking lots of pictures ☐
12 preparing the models ☐

6 **2.13** Listen again. What were the speakers referring to when they used the following adjectives?

1 important _____
2 good _____
3 bad _____
4 freezing _____
5 starving _____
6 terrible _____
7 fascinating _____

GRAMMAR: ungradable adjectives

7 Complete the table.

Gradable	Ungradable
angry	*furious*
	excellent
	essential
	unique
bad	
interesting	
big	
	starving
small	
	exhausted
	devastated
cold	

8 Change the underlined adjectives to either gradable or ungradable.

Last night, rescue teams saved Cassandra Morley and her friends, who spent two nights in ¹ cold conditions. The ² tired group of teenagers were returned to their ³ upset parents this morning. However, the ⁴ furious chief of the Rescue Team described the teenagers as 'irresponsible'. 'This is not a ⁵ unique occurrence in this area. However, it is ⁶ important that people remember to respect this part of the country. It can be very dangerous indeed,' he said.

9 Complete the sentences with the adverbs in the box. Use each adverb once only.

slightly   absolutely   very
really   extremely   bit

1 I had a _____ good time. Thank you.
2 That was the worst film I have ever seen. It was _____ terrible!
3 The lecture was _____ interesting. Now I want to find out more!
4 I'm a _____ hungry but I can wait.
5 The ring is _____ small for me. Could you make it a little bigger?
6 The hill is _____ enormous! I can't climb that!

DICTATION

1 [2.14] Listen and write what you hear.

_____

_____

_____

_____

_____

_____

_____

READING

2 Read the article. Choose from the list A–F the sentence which best summarises each part of the article.

A Hirst believes that other people can do the work but he is still the artist. ____

B Charles Saatchi has been a big influence on Hirst's success. ____

C His best known work shows an interest in the subject of Death. ____

D Since he finished working with Saatchi, Hirst has continued to be successful. ____

E Many people do not believe that Hirst is an artist. ____

F Hirst has made a lot of money from his art. ____

Damien Hirst – Artist or Entrepreneur?

1 Born in Bristol on 7 June 1965, Damien Hirst is the best known member of the group that has been called the 'Young British Artists'. Damien became known after the collector Charles Saatchi started supporting his work. His work was first shown in 1992 in the first Young British Artists exhibition at the Saatchi Gallery in North London. Throughout the nineties, it was Saatchi's support that certainly contributed to Hirst's success.

2 Hirst's first major work was titled _The Physical Impossibility of Death in the Mind of Someone Living_ and was a large dead tiger shark in formaldehyde* in a glass tank. Death is a central theme in Hirst's work. He is mostly known for his Natural History series, in which dead animals (such as a shark, a sheep or a cow) are preserved, sometimes cut-up, in formaldehyde.

3 The sale of this work, in 2004, made him the second most expensive living artist. In June 2007, Hirst became the most expensive living artist with the sale of a medicine chest, _Lullaby Spring_, for £9.65m at Sotheby's in London.

4 What makes Hirst so controversial is that he is often accused of becoming successful because of work done by other people. It is true that he has many assistants working with him and Hirst believes their work is also his work. This is because he sees the real creative act as being the idea, not the actual making of the piece. Therefore, it is the creator of the idea who is the artist.

> ... _he sees the real creative act as being the idea, not the actual making of the piece._

5 There has also been much discussion on whether Hirst's work is art or not. One critic has said that a stuffed animal on the wall is more art than the work of Hirst. There is also a group of artists who are against the work of Hirst. Called the Stuckists, in 2003 they opened an exhibition which showed a shark in the window of the front of a shop. Named _A Dead Shark Isn't Art_, the Stuckists showed that this was a real shop window that Hirst may have often walked past at some time in his life before creating _The Physical Impossibility_ ...

6 Regardless of such criticism and despite the breakdown of the relationship between Saatchi and Hirst, the artist's popularity continues to grow steadily. In May 2007, an exhibition of Hirst's new work presented _For The Love of God_, a human skull recreated in platinum and covered with 8,601 diamonds. Approximately £15m worth of diamonds were used. On 30 August 2007, Hirst outdid his previous sale of _Lullaby Spring_ when _For The Love of God_ was sold for £50m to an unknown investment group.

* Formaldehyde is a gas used with water to preserve dead things.

The Physical Impossibility of Death in the Mind of Someone Living – by Damien Hirst

3 Read the article again. What do the following numbers or dates refer to?

1 9.65 million _____

2 8,601 _____

3 1965 _____

4 50 million _____

5 1992 _____

**VOCABULARY:
order of adjectives**

4 Read the example phrases. Tick the descriptions that correctly describe the order of adjectives.

lovely, old, green, silk scarf

small, antique, Turkish tea glass

expensive, tiny, green, African emerald

a large, dead tiger shark

1 Age comes before material.

2 Nationality comes before size.

3 Opinion comes after material.

4 Size comes before colour.

5 Function comes just before the noun.

5 Correct these noun phrases.

1 a green large Spanish cotton shirt

_____

2 the well-known beautiful ballet Italian dancer

_____

3 a travelling enormous well-dressed German salesman

_____

4 a metal expensive large Swiss silver wrist watch

_____

**GRAMMAR:
position of adverbs**

6 Look at the article on page 63 and find one example of each of the different types of adverbs.

1 adverb of time: _____

2 adverb of certainty: _____

3 adverb of place: _____

4 adverb of frequency: _____

5 adverb of degree: _____

6 adverb of manner: _____

7 Choose the best answer a, b, c or d, to complete the sentences.

1 The exhibition took place ____.

   a) to Leeds   c) in June

   b) certainly   d) mostly

2 We ____ take the tram to school.

   a) usually   c) then

   b) carefully   d) completely

3 He left the sculptures ____.

   a) probably   c) then

   b) creatively   d) at home

4 They are ____ worth that much money.

   a) there   c) frequently

   b) mainly   d) certainly

5 He threw the flowers to the floor ____.

   a) probably   c) dramatically

   b) mostly   d) often

6 He ____ works on Tuesdays but occasionally on Saturdays.

   a) certainly   c) then

   b) mostly   d) quickly

SCENARIO: The new exhibition

LISTENING

1 `2.15` **Listen to the presentation and choose the correct answer a, b or c.**

1 The talk is about

   a) a doctor.

   b) a student.

   c) a candidate for a job.

2 The person who is talking is probably

   a) a member of the department.

   b) a student.

   c) a friend of the candidate.

3 How does the speaker feel?

   a) that he is perfect

   b) that he is not the right person

   c) she is not completely happy with the choice

KEY LANGUAGE: sequencing information, moving to a new point

2 `2.15` **Listen again and put the phrases in the order you hear them.**

a) OK, that's it for … ____

b) Finally, I'll … ____

c) Let's go on to … ____

d) Right, I've told you … ____

e) OK, that's all I have … ____

f) First, I'll … ____

g) So moving … ____

h) Right, now you know … ____

3a `2.16` Listen and complete the phrases.

a) OK, that's it for _____.

b) Finally, I'll _____.

c) Let's go on to _____.

d) Right, I've told you _____.

e) OK, that's all I have _____.

f) First, I'll _____.

g) So moving _____.

h) Right, now you know _____.

3b **Put the phrases in the correct group.**

1 ordering information in a talk

2 signalling the end of a topic

3 changing to a new topic

STUDY SKILLS: expanding your vocabulary

1 **Match pairs of adjectives.**

1 absurd

2 exhilarating

3 humorous

4 monotonous

5 heartbreaking

6 absorbing

7 appalling

8 brilliant

a) compelling

b) tedious

c) terrific

d) gripping

e) witty

f) dreadful

g) ridiculous

h) touching

2 **Replace the adverb in each sentence with another adverb that means the same thing.**

1 The exhibition can generally be seen in the Red Room. _____

2 The house was completely destroyed in the earthquake. _____

3 Don't worry. He will certainly call you this evening. _____

4 It is a particularly difficult job to collect samples in this weather. _____

5 I really had no idea that you were coming. _____

3 Complete the text with the right adverb or adjective in the box.

dreadful	particularly	witty	ridiculous
certainly	touching	brilliant	truly
absorbing	totally	gripping	tedious

THE ARTS CENTRE
This Week

It's a ¹_____ good week at the Arts Centre this week as there are a lot of new things happening.

. . . .

THE GREEN ROOM

This week the Green Room is showing some of the work of Damien Hirst. His ²_____ work, ³_____ the best the UK has to offer the art world, is a must see. Some have called his work ⁴_____. They argue that it doesn't have the right to be called 'art' but I suggest you go along yourself and find out. There are also some ⁵_____ new works being shown for the first time. Unfortunately the Green Room is only showing his work for one week, which is a ⁶_____ decision in my opinion. They should have it for at least three weeks.

. . . .

THE THEATRE

The local theatre group is presenting that ⁷_____ classic by William Shakespeare, 'Romeo and Juliet'. I challenge you not to cry! It's also really ⁸_____, especially the great fight scenes! The performances of Peter Allan and Sherry Taylor as Romeo and Juliet are ⁹_____ superb.

. . . .

THE SMALL ROOM

This week the comedienne, Paula Platt is presenting her one-woman show 'Why I gave it all up'. Some people think she is very ¹⁰_____ and there is certainly a lot of laughter at her shows. However, I find her rather ¹¹_____ — every joke sounds the same to me.

. . . .

THE CINEMA

This week, because of popular demand, the cinema is showing the documentary 'A Life in a Day' again. This look at the work of doctors and nurses in wartime is so ¹²_____. One hour seemed to pass in five minutes.

WRITING SKILLS:
an online review

4 Read the notes about one of the following week's activities at the Arts Centre. Using the review in Exercise 3 as a model, write a review for 'Where's my husband gone?' Use different adjectives or adverbs.

The Theatre - humorous musical 'where's my husband gone?' Musical written by terrific writer Sam Shaw ... also wrote 'The Last Song of Summer' one of most heart-breaking plays ever written. Was looking forward to this. However completely disappointed. Musical rather monotonous as things happen very slowly. The director Peter Apted doesn't know what doing. Musical's set in Paris but stage design was laughable - didn't look like Paris at all. Performance by Diane Cather really dreadful. Would not recommend to anyone except lovers of appalling theatre. Better to go to interesting exhibition of Ribienko's paintings.

_____

_____

_____

_____

_____

_____

_____

_____

Romeo and Juliet

Psychology

10.1 GROUP PSYCHOLOGY

VOCABULARY: words from the lesson

1a Write the adjective form of these nouns.

1 practicality _____

2 resourcefulness _____

3 conscientiousness _____

4 creativity _____

5 energy _____

6 knowledge _____

7 ambition _____

8 authority _____

9 diplomacy _____

10 objectivity _____

1b Match the adjectives above with the following definitions.

a) determined to be successful, rich, powerful, etc. ____

b) behaving or speaking in a confident, determined way that makes people respect and obey you ____

c) careful to do everything that it is your job or duty to do ____

d) involving the use of imagination to produce new ideas or things ____

e) dealing with people politely and skilfully without upsetting them ____

f) having lots of physical and mental strength to do things ____

g) having information, skills, and understanding through learning or experience ____

h) able to make a decision that is based on facts rather than on your feelings or beliefs ____

i) good at dealing with problems and making decisions based on what is possible and what will really work ____

j) good at coming up with creative solutions to problems in any situation ____

VOCABULARY: working together

2 Complete the verbs in the text with prepositions.

When Stephanie and Marco broke ¹_____ it meant that Marco had managed to fall ²_____ with all his friends. Nobody likes to break a friendship, but Marco is so bad-tempered and cynical that it is impossible to spend more than five minutes with him. Personally, I was surprised that Stephanie put ³_____ with it for so long. He is so difficult to get ⁴_____ with!

Anyway, I think Marco needs to get ⁵_____ to learning some interpersonal skills otherwise he'll have to get used ⁶_____ being lonely.

TRANSLATION

3 Translate the verbs from Exercise 2 into your language.

1 _____

2 _____

3 _____

4 _____

5 _____

6 _____

VOCABULARY: idioms

1 Complete the idioms connected with *mind*.

1 Is it true, you're going to do a bungee jump? Are you _____ mind?

2 It's time you _____ mind about the job offer.

3 You cannot take sides in this negotiation. You need _____ mind.

4 Now that she knows they will help, she will have considerable _____ mind.

5 The government seems _____ minds about the environment. I wish they'd decide.

DICTATION

2a [2.17] Listen and write what you hear.

_____

_____

_____

_____

_____

_____

_____

_____

2b Read what you have written and decide what the paragraph is describing.

a) a fear   b) an allergy   c) a phobia

READING

READ BETTER

There are three ways in which we order a passage:
CHRONOLOGICAL This is ordering the paragraphs according to time. This is mostly done when telling a story. The older the information, the earlier it comes in a paragraph.
SPATIAL This is generally used when describing things. For example, when describing a room, you describe the room from right to left, far to near or front to back.
LOGICAL This is the most common, and used for all other texts. Usually this will mean moving from general to specific.

3 Read the following paragraphs that continue the dictation and put them in the correct order.

1 ___ 2 ___ 3 ___ 4 ___ 5 ___ 6 ___

A It is generally recognised that there are two steps in the treatment of phobias. The first step involves the victim coming face-to-face with the phobia. For example, someone who has a phobia of flying will start using the following hierarchy: watching a video about the safety of flying, meeting frequent flyers, visiting a plane when it is on the ground, experiencing a short flight.

B Finally, it is important for victims of phobias to remember that a phobia is a normal condition. A person with a phobia may rarely come into contact with the cause of their phobia and will normally behave in exactly the same way as everyone else.

C As well as there not necessarily being a reason for the phobia, it is true that the victim only needs to anticipate the situation in which the phobia may take place. This will most often result in anxiety-related physical occurrences, such as an increased heart rate, a loss of breath, sweating, trembling, pain in the stomach or worse.

D A second step is to deal with the thoughts that people have, which cause the physical responses to the phobia. This is done by finding positive responses to these thoughts. Instead of thinking 'This plane will crash', they should think 'This is the safest way to travel'.

E There are three types of phobias. Firstly, there is agoraphobia, which is the only condition that can be treated by doctors. This is a fear of leaving home or leaving a place that feels safe. The second type is social phobias, which involve the victim with other people or in social situations which are potentially embarrassing. For example, someone with a strong phobia for speaking in public may be physically incapable of opening their mouth. Finally, there are specific phobias. These phobias are usually caused by a single event or thing and can be very strange. For example, people who go into a panic attack if they see a clown or a vegetable. As these are really unique and so different from each other, they require a different treatment for each one, which makes correct identification of phobias especially important.

F Although this two-step process is considered very successful in treating phobias, some phobias are stronger than others and it may never be possible to overcome them.

GRAMMAR:
relative clauses

5a Find and underline relative clauses in the dictation and the reading text.

5b Mark each relative clause as D (defining) or N (non-defining).

6 Complete the sentences with a relative pronoun.

1 What was the number of the room in _____ he was staying?

2 He is the man _____ you need to see.

3 Do you know _____ he will have his appointment?

4 Dr Lloyd was the person with _____ he was speaking.

5 His phobia seems to be weakening, _____ is very good news.

6 I really couldn't tell you _____ car that is. I know it's not mine.

7 They are staying at the Limewold Hotel, _____ won Best Hotel of the Year last year.

7 Rewrite each set of sentences as one sentence containing a defining or non-defining relative clause.

1 He couldn't get on the plane. It was a real disappointment.

_____

2 Simon is staying overnight in the hospital. He had a panic attack today.

_____

3 Victims could find themselves in situations. These situations could cause the phobia.

_____

4 He suffers from agoraphobia. This means he should see a doctor.

_____

5 This is the play. In this play Steven Jones gave his greatest performance.

_____

6 A man helped us last week. Do you know his name?

_____

4 Are these sentences true or false, according to the text?

1 The victim needs to experience the phobia in order to deal with it.

2 Thinking positively does not help people with phobias.

3 Two types of phobia can be treated by doctors.

4 All phobias can be cured.

5 People can experience a phobia just by thinking about it.

6 There is not always a reason for a phobia.

VOCABULARY: psychology

1 Complete the text with the words in the box.

> deduce   profiles   assessments   motives
> psychiatrist   case files

Callan University – Psychology Club

Wednesday 25 March 2008 19.30

**Q&A Session –
Special Guest: Dr Elfman**

Title: Lying. Good or Bad?

Dr Elfman, daughter of the great ¹_____ Dr Holgar Elfman, is senior lecturer in psychology at Tilberg University. Prior to working at Tilberg, she was a criminal psychologist providing ²_____ of criminals to help police solve the most complex of crimes. She has spent the last six months researching the issue of lying, specifically what ³_____ people give for lying. So far, she has put together more than 500 ⁴_____ on pathological liars, leading psychologists to ⁵_____ that there may be more than just socio-cultural reasons behind why people lie. She has recently opened her own company which provides staff ⁶_____ of major companies and organisations.

---

2 Read the text again and answer the questions.

1 What is the purpose of the text?

   a) to give information about Dr Elfman

   b) to discuss research on lying

   c) to advertise an event

2 As well as working at the university, what does Dr Elfman do?

   _____

3 What evidence have scientists used to prove that there may be more than socio-cultural reasons behind why people lie?

   _____

LISTENING

3 [2.18] Listen to the Q&A session and tick the topics that are discussed.

1 What makes people lie?

2 Are there unique psychical characteristics that show someone is lying?

3 Scientists lie.

4 Some businesses value liars.

5 What is a lie?

6 Is lying a skill?

7 People lie in business because they are told to.

8 Why do liars sound too good to be true?

4 [2.18] Listen again and choose the correct answer a, b or c.

1 Dr Elfman believes it

   a) is easy to know when someone is lying.

   b) is sometimes difficult to be sure when someone is lying.

   c) is impossible to be sure when someone is lying.

2 Which physical reaction do most people expect from liars?

   a) They can't sit in one place.

   b) They touch their noses.

   c) They don't look at the listener.

3 Why could liars be valued by businesses?

   a) They can sell things more easily.

   b) They can make people redundant.

   c) They are useful in marketing.

4 What does Dr Elfman say about some characteristics that liars do have?

   a) They are not only common in liars.

   b) If liars have them, they are skilful.

   c) They show that their speech is unplanned.

GRAMMAR: reduced relative clauses

5a 2.19 Listen and complete the sentences.

1 We're lucky to have with us tonight, Dr Sarah Elfman, _____ from Tilburg University, and Director of Management Profilers UK.

2 The majority of people _____ 'How can you tell when people are lying', insisted that liars avoid looking at you.

3 The result _____ into the behaviour of lying is that, in fact, there is no physical reaction to help the listener deduce that the speaker is lying.

4 Is it a lie if you try and convince someone that the product _____ is the best on the market …

5 Well, even liars _____ tend to overdo it.

6 It also seems to be the case _____ a lot more body language.

5b Which of the sentences are reduced relative clauses? How do you know?

EXTRA LANGUAGE: more about reduced relative clauses

You cannot reduce a relative clause if it is followed by an adjective or a noun, e.g. *The woman who is unhappy is my mother* cannot become ~~The woman unhappy is my mother~~. Likewise, *The woman who is the nurse is my mother* cannot become ~~The woman the nurse is my mother~~.

You cannot reduce a relative clause if the relative pronoun is the object. *This is the picture that I told you about* cannot become ~~This is the picture told you about~~.

6 Which of these sentences can be reduced? Underline the words that would need to change and write the correct participle.

1 Make sure you follow the recipe <u>that is given</u> at the top of the page. *given*

2 The car which was sold yesterday cost £50,000.

3 There are serious issues that face the new president.

4 The man who is staying upstairs is a famous writer.

5 The Andes is a mountain range that covers a large area in South America.

6 The coat which I bought my daughter is very warm.

7 I recently heard about a dog who was bitten by a man.

7 Rewrite the sentences using a reduced relative clause. One sentence cannot be changed.

1 People who walk on the grass will be prosecuted.

2 The book that was borrowed from the library went missing.

3 It was a big accident which resulted in many deaths.

4 The car that was damaged in the accident is mine.

5 He could have read the report that I wrote.

6 He stole the money, which gave us no option but to ask him to leave.

7 The man who is the security guard is my cousin.

8 I need to look at the books that are located on the first floor.

KEY LANGUAGE: giving advice

1a Complete the sentences with the phrases in the box.

why don't you	it might be	advise you to
think you need	might consider	vital that
could also	it's essential	if I were you

a) I would also _____ be careful when you talk to him. ☐

b) You _____ moving him into Sales. ☐

c) I _____ to talk to her about it first. ☐

d) Well, _____, the first thing that I would do is change the Marketing Manager. ☐

e) _____ talk to Bill first? ☐

f) It's _____ you make the changes soon. ☐

g) You _____ offer him some time away from the office. ☐

h) _____ that a Marketing Manager is respected by the team. ☐

i) However, _____ a good idea to keep it confidential. ☐

1b `2.20` Listen and check your answers.

2 `2.20` Listen again. Put the sentences in the order you hear them.

PRONUNCIATION

3 `2.21` Listen and practise saying the sentences. Which words are stressed?

1 _____

2 _____

3 _____

4 _____

5 _____

6 _____

WRITING SKILLS: a discursive essay

1 Read the essay and underline the correct linking words.

When a child is due, most potential mothers need to take time off work to have their children. Once this maternity leave finishes, the mother is faced with a decision to go back to work or to stay at home with her child. This essay looks at the arguments for and against mothers staying at home to look after their children.

[1] *In addition / A major advantage / Another advantage* of staying at home is that it strengthens the relationship between mother and child. Recent psychological studies have suggested that this not only helps the child to develop psychologically, for example by having increased confidence and being better able to show affection, but also physically. [2] *However / In addition / On the other hand*, the relationship between mother and child also strengthens the idea of family in the child and promotes a better attitude to responsibility. [3] *As a result / On the other hand / Another advantage* of mothers staying at home, it is suggested, is that the child's education is accelerated. Mothers who stay at home seem to take an active role in their children's education and because all parents are ambitious for their children they are more motivated than, say, a nanny. [4] *As a result / In addition / Therefore*, according to recent studies, children of parents who stay at home start reading much earlier than children who are looked after by a person outside the family. Children whose mothers stay at home, [5] *however / another advantage / therefore* seem to have an advantage psychologically, physically and in terms of education.

[6] *On the other hand / Moreover / A major adavantage*, there are financial issues to consider. It is a fact that many families cannot afford to have one parent stay at home. The loss of one income in a society where both parents' incomes are substantial can result in serious financial difficulties for the family. It is true that a nanny isn't cheap, but they are usually less of a problem than the loss of a whole salary. [7] *As a result / Therefore / Furthermore*, it can be argued that parents need their jobs. In today's society both men and women are equally ambitious. It can be psychologically damaging for a mother to give up her ambitions to stay at home. [8] *However / Moreover / Another advantage*, it can result in a lessening of self-confidence and an increase in depression. [9] *Furthermore / However / Therefore*, at the same time it can be argued that looking after a child is the one time when a mother must show self-satisfaction, self-confidence and love to their child.

3 To summarise, the advantages of a parent staying at home seem to support the development of a child. However, some parents may not choose to do this because they cannot make the financial sacrifice necessary, nor can one parent comfortably deal with the loss of ambition. Parents should try to create a situation where there is a member of the family at home as, in my opinion, the young child must come first.

2b What were the two things you checked for to make your decision?

1 _____

2 _____

STUDY SKILLS: writing a bibliography, referencing

3 Make the necessary changes to the bibliography that goes with the essay.

1 Prentice Hall New York Chris Smith 2003 Mothers and Home

_____

2 The Maternity Journal vol 26 2004 Helen Szulc pp.123–176 Where does Mummy go now?

_____

3 Last accessed 2005 12 June 2008 http://www. aclu/ psychology/motherschildren/archive Mother & Baby Research

_____

2a Look at these three possible conclusions and decide which one is best.

1 To sum up, the main advantages of staying at home are the strengthening of the relationship between mother and child, the strengthening of the idea of family and therefore responsibility and an increase in the education of the child. The disadvantages are the financial situation and the psychological damage it can do to mothers. In my opinion it is clear that mothers should therefore go back to work.

2 In conclusion, it is quite clear that there are advantages for the mother staying at home, especially for the child and disadvantages, especially for the parents and, specifically the mother. If we also include the fact that there has been an increase in crime related to children being left alone and outside help entering the home, it seems logical to me that one parent should stay at home with the child.

Cultures

11.1 DEFINING CULTURE

READING

1 Read the article. Who refers to the following aspects of culture? Write A, B, C or D.

1 Geography (x2) ___, ___

2 Life rituals ___

3 Architecture ___

4 Values ___

5 Climate ___

6 Customs and traditions (x3) ___, ___, ___

7 Institutions ___

8 Historical events ___

9 Rules of behaviour ___

10 Cuisine ___

11 Religion ___

A George

Our capital city sums up our culture. London's skyline is justly famous for the different buildings that can be seen such as the Post Office Tower, the 'Gherkin' and The Tower of London to name just a few. Finally, there is Big Ben and the Houses of Parliament where the government is based. England does have a monarchy but it is really the government that is in power. London's particularly great on 5th November when we celebrate Guy Fawkes Night. This was the night in 1605 when Guy Fawkes tried to blow up Parliament. On that night every year the sky around London is full of fireworks.

C Helen

The Isles of Scilly is not really a different country but it certainly is a different way of life and that life is controlled by the world around us. Our islands are not very inviting. They are very rocky with lots of hills and valleys and it is almost impossible to get away from the sea. It is also very, very windy here because it is the place where the Atlantic begins. However, it is also very beautiful and the summers are great. On the Isles of Scilly we believe in living close to nature. We still live a quite traditional life on the island and we take great care to preserve the natural character of the islands.

B Yoshi

Because our country is a group of islands, most of our food comes from the sea and we are particularly famous for our raw fish. Noodles and rice are also important. Japanese food has changed very little through the ages. For example, it is still considered correct to eat with chopsticks rather than a knife and a fork. It is also expected that before we start eating we say 'itadakimasu'. We even say it to ourselves when we are alone. English people can find this strange when eating with us. There is no translation really, the best being 'I shall receive' but that doesn't mean much I suppose.

D Veera

The Hindu calendar is full of holidays. Maybe it's because we have so many gods! Anyway, some of our festivals involve dancing, especially Navaratri when we dance the Garba. This is a time I really love. Another is Hindu weddings because they are so complex. There are so many different things that have to be done. My sister is getting married next and I have so many responsibilities. I don't know how I'll manage.

VOCABULARY: words from the lesson

2 Fill the gaps with one word. The first letter is given to help you.

1 The t_____ around the lake is quite hilly so make sure you've got good walking boots.

2 Showing the bottom of your feet to people is considered very bad m_____ in Asia.

3 Although it is a ruin, the castle is protected as it is part of our national h_____.

4 He may be English but his d_____ is so strange that I don't understand anything!

5 What did you do on your wedding a_____?

6 It's just a s_____ that a red sky at night will mean a beautiful day tomorrow.

7 He has joined a religious s_____ that believes that we all come from another planet.

8 You should also include green vegetables as part of your s_____ diet.

DICTATION

1a `2.22` **Listen and write what you hear.**

Coal, Frankincense and Myrrh, a major new exhibition at Sheffield's Weston Park Museum.

_____

_____

_____

_____

_____

_____

_____

_____

_____

1b **Read what you wrote and choose the correct answer a, b or c.**

1 Where can you find this type of text?

a) in a report

b) in a review

c) on a poster

2 What did the Yemenis do first?

a) worked as painters

b) worked as sailors

c) worked in factories

3 Which of the following things will you <u>not</u> see at the exhibition?

a) things Yemenis believe in

b) the important times in a Yemeni's life

c) examples of Yemeni art

LISTENING

2 `2.23` **Listen. Where did these things happen? Write Y (Yemen) or U (UK).**

1 Eman opened the door to see her father. ____

2 People slept in the same beds. ____

3 He decided to leave a large family. ____

4 Language classes are organised. ____

5 They visited English Yemenis. ____

6 The man started crying. ____

3 `2.23` **Listen again and tick the facts about Yemenis that are true.**

1 They used to send cards and pictures to their families. ____

2 People thought life would be better in the UK. ____

3 They were paid very well. ____

4 They have their own sports centre in Sheffield. ____

5 They find it difficult to go back and live in Yemen.

____

GRAMMAR: reported speech

4a `2.24` **Listen and fill the gaps in these sentences.**

1 I opened the door for him and _____ _____ he was.

2 When he _____ my dad, he hugged me and I was really shy.

3 One man who went back to Yemen _____ like a foreigner in his own country.

4 He mentioned the town of Underfield to one man, and this man _____.

4b **Match the sentences above with a–c.**

a) reported *yes/no* questions

b) reported statements

c) reported questions

5a Rewrite the sentences from the listening as reported speech.

1 'I started to forget what he looked like.'

She said _____

2 'Some people find it difficult to resolve their cultural identity.'

He said _____

3 'Our community association runs an advice centre.'

He said _____.

4 'I'm planning to take my family there little things from England.'

She said _____.

5 'Your husband is English.'

He said _____.

6 'Has he been to Yemen with you?'

He asked _____.

7 'You went back to Yemen when you retired.'

He said _____.

8 'I have become part of the community here.'

He said _____.

5b Which three sentences above do not change the tense of the verb? Why not?

1 _____

2 _____

3 _____

6 Complete the text about how Radhi felt when he first came to England. Use the adjectives in the box.

| stimulated isolated inadequate |
| frustrated hostile intriguing |

When I first arrived in England I didn't feel
¹_____ because we came in a big group so I had my friends to stop me feeling lonely. Rather it was an ²_____ adventure because I knew nothing about England and I felt ³_____ and wanted to learn the language as quickly as possible. When I arrived my English was worse than ⁴_____ – I couldn't say anything! Although sometimes I got ⁵_____ because I couldn't say what I wanted, the English were always very helpful. They were never ⁶_____ to me.

EXTRA VOCABULARY: word formation

7 Complete the table. Use a dictionary to help you.

Noun	Verb	Adjective	Adverb
		stimulated	✗
		isolated	✗
	✗	inadequate	
		frustrated	✗
	✗	hostile	✗
	✗	intriguing	

8 Complete the same table as Exercise 7, but in your language. Do you use the same words for each meaning? How do they change?

Noun	Verb	Adjective	Adverb
			✗
			✗
	✗		
			✗
	✗		
	✗		

READING

1 Read the text. Tick the statements you can infer from the text.

1 This is preparation for a lecture.

2 The students have to complete a task before the next lesson.

3 The writer provides ways to understand differences between cultures.

4 The characteristics show that some cultures are better than others.

5 The categories will help students to complete their task.

READ BETTER

Sometimes completing an activity does not require you to read the whole text. First skim the text and make sure you understand the general meaning of each section. Then read each question. What are the key words in the question and which section do you think they refer to? In this way you save time. Remember when you read you are looking for the information you need. Most of the time, when we read to gather information, we do not need to read every word.

HOFSTEDE'S FRAMEWORK FOR ASSESSING CULTURES

1 *Small or Large Power Distance*
Hofstede defines this as the way people in a culture see and respect the differences in power between, for example, managers and workers. For instance, in a small power distance culture, people have a more democratic system where one person does not have all the power. In large power difference cultures, people expect to see managers behaving like father figures. They do not criticise decisions made by their managers. An example of a small power distance culture might be seen in Denmark, whilst an example of a large power distance culture might be seen in China.

2 *Individualism versus Collectivism*
How do people see themselves in a culture? Are they an important member of a team or just individuals? People in an individualistic culture will think of themselves first. In collectivist cultures, for example, family or friends or even colleagues may come first. Collectivism may be seen in Latin America and more individualism may be seen in the USA.

3 *Masculinity versus Femininity*
Put simply, it is really a choice between quantity of life and quality of life. A masculine culture may consider competition and ambition important values and success may be evaluated by the amount of money or possessions you have. A feminine culture may put more value on relationships and the quality of life. More masculine characteristics may be seen in countries like Japan whereas more feminine characteristics may be seen in Sweden.

4 *Uncertainty Avoidance*
Are people comfortable with uncertainty or does it make them anxious? Cultures that have high uncertainty avoidance are cultures with lots of social rules and traditions and where people stay in one job longer.

CLASS C&C103

For your first assignment, you are expected to carry out research using Hofstede's questionnaire to discover the dominant values in different cultures. Geert Hofstede is an important writer whose books are about cultures and organisational cultures. He suggests that common beliefs in a culture may affect the way people work with others. He uses five different categories (see attached) to show this. Use the categories and the questionnaire to question fifteen foreign students at the university and then report back, for the next class, what you found out.

REMEMBER: Hofstede does not use these characteristics to describe the culture of a country. They are usually only used to help people understand how people may work in different countries.

Dr Anderton

Usually this means that everyone knows the practices and the traditions and life does not have much uncertainty. High uncertainty avoidance may be seen more often in Mediterranean countries. Low uncertainty avoidance may be seen more in Northern European countries where people are always changing jobs and working with few rules.

5 *Long- versus Short-term Orientation*
Long-term cultures look to the future so will value the skills of saving money, patience and dealing with things in a sensible and practical way. Short-term cultures value tradition and the giving and receiving of gifts and favours. Short-term orientation may be seen more in Asian countries, whilst western countries might have more examples of long-term orientation.

2 Read the text again. Which of Hofstede's characteristics is being described in each person's behaviour?

1 He doesn't go out because he wants to save money to buy a house.

_____

2 She's been offered a much better job but she is afraid to leave the job she knows.

_____

3 She's just bought a Ferrari. She only bought it because Sarah bought a new car last week.

_____

4 She gave up her place at university to look after her grandmother.

_____

5 They don't like their group leader because he doesn't discuss issues with them before making a decision.

_____

LISTENING

3 **2.25** Listen to the discussion between two students and check your answers to Exercise 2.

GRAMMAR: reporting verbs

4 **2.25** Listen again and write down all the reporting verbs you hear.

_____

_____

5 Match the reporting verbs 1–8 with the structure that follows them a–c.

1 encourage ____ 5 regret ____

2 promise ____ 6 admit ____

3 invite ____ 7 persuade ____

4 apologise for ____ 8 agree ____

a) infinitive with *to*

b) object + infinitive with *to*

c) *-ing* form

6 Choose the right reporting verb a, b, or c to complete the sentences.

1 The accused ____ breaking into the house at three o'clock in the morning.

a) admitted   b) refused   c) told

2 They have ____ making too much noise last night.

a) warned   b) apologised for   c) refused

3 We have been ____ him to take the job.

a) offering   b) insisting on   c) encouraging

4 Did you ____ him to take his shoes off when he enters their house?

a) admit   b) warn   c) offer

5 They ____ to re-enter into negotiations with us.

a) refused   b) regretted   c) encouraged

7 Fill the gaps with the verb in brackets in the correct form. You may also need to add an object.

Our son is a big disappointment. We have always tried to help him but he seems unable to take life seriously. For example, when the Hamlyn Corporation invited ¹_____ (work) with them we promised ²_____ (support) him. We encouraged ³_____ (take) evening classes in accounting and even paid for them. Two weeks later he asked for more money for the course. When he admitted ⁴_____ (spend) the money on going out with his friends we were very disappointed, even though he offered ⁵_____ (pay) us back. We were not surprised when he lost the job. They had told ⁶_____ (improve) his work many times but he had ignored them. I think we both regret ⁷_____ (support) him now.

KEY LANGUAGE: creating impact in a presentation

1a `2.26` **Listen and complete the extracts.**

1 Culture represents _____ _____ of a group of people, whether it is a nation or a small community.

2 OK, so what _____?

3 Turning now to the next part, _____ _____?

4 … as one culture becomes more influential, it becomes _____ to convince younger people to keep to their culture.

5 So, in conclusion, culture is important to people as it describes where they come from, _____ they are going to.

6 Thanks to the work of cultural organisations around the world _____ being protected …

7 What I think is needed is more cultural support _____ on the streets …

1b **Organise the extracts above into three groups.**

Repetition	Tripling	Rhetorical questions
4		

STUDY SKILLS: improving reading skills

1a **Match the prefixes with the words.**

1	anti	a)	national
2	counter	b)	war
3	inter	c)	cultural
4	mis	d)	culture
5	multi	e)	understanding
6	post	f)	social
7	pre	g)	culture
8	sub	h)	date

1b **Complete the sentences with words from above.**

1 I think there has been a _____. I said we'd be here by six, not seven.

2 Within the teenage culture we can find the gothic _____ whose members tend to dress in black.

3 When you answer a question with a single-word answer it suggests that you are an _____ person as you do not wish to communicate.

4 With so many people from different countries living in England, it is true to say that it has become _____.

5 I've always been interested in how countries talk to each other so I am going to study _____ relations.

2 **Match the root of each word with its meaning, then add the relevant suffix.**

1 valu_____

2 respons_____

3 time_____

4 communicat_____

5 develop_____

6 sex_____

7 socio_____

a) how people interact

b) the belief that one sex is weaker than the other

c) can be trusted to do things when asked

d) the study of society and the behaviour of people

e) worth a lot of money

f) the process by which we try and improve

g) can last forever

3 Complete the text with the expressions in the box.

> on the contrary   alternatively   provided that
> in addition   similarly   nevertheless
> in order to   therefore

I have not always been a follower of tradition.
¹_____, when I was young I did
everything I could to break away from our traditions.
²_____ to avoiding traditions, I also
criticised them to my foreign friends. However,
I became defensive when they criticised them.
Criticism was fine, ³_____ it was done
by me. ⁴_____, it came as a surprise that
as I got older I came to value our traditions more.
⁵_____, I became more concerned
about family and bringing up children into a life that
was safe. Some people say that ⁶_____
really appreciate your life you need to grow old. This
is true, if you are lucky enough to have children.
⁷_____, you may have nieces or
nephews that you care about. As we all get
older, most of us want families; it should,
⁸_____, not be surprising that we
become traditionalists.

WRITING SKILLS: a formal letter

4 Put the words in the correct order to make phrases or sentences from a formal letter.

1 copy of please enclosed CV my find a

_____

2 your advertisement writing with to I reference am

_____

3 the above can I be any at at email address time contacted

_____

4 the abroad travelling question regarding of …

_____

5 any can if I further be of assistance, hesitate contact please do to me not

_____

6 forward in the I future look to you from near hearing

_____

5 Use the phrases and sentences in Exercise 4 to write a formal letter of application for a job. Make sure you use the correct layout for your letter.

_____

_____

_____

_____

_____

_____

_____

_____

_____

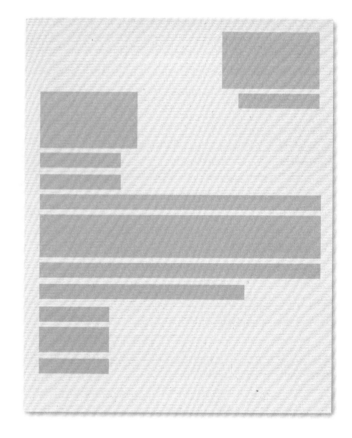

12.1 DEVICES AND GADGETS

VOCABULARY: technology

1 Match the words with the definitions.

1 technological

2 appliance

3 device

4 engine

5 equipment

6 gadget

7 machine

8 technology

9 technophobe

a) new machines, equipment and ways of doing things that are based on modern knowledge about science and computers

b) a piece of equipment, especially electrical equipment, such as a cooker or washing machine, used in people's homes

c) the tools, machines, clothes, etc. that you need to do a particular job or activity

d) a small, useful, and cleverly-designed machine or tool

e) someone who does not like modern machines, such as computers, and would prefer to live without them

f) adjective – related to technology

g) a machine or tool that does a special job

h) the part of a vehicle that produces power to make it move

i) a piece of equipment with moving parts that uses power such as electricity to do a particular job

2 Put the letters in the correct order to make adjectives that describe technology.

1 hrda-wreaing _____

2 ttngicu eged _____

3 esolobte _____

4 esya ot sue _____

5 atste-fo-the-rat _____

6 radblue _____

7 viroallyenmentn ynldreif _____

8 uot fo etda _____

9 reus-dlfeirny _____

10 reeng _____

11 dnhay _____

12 clarticap _____

3 Complete the text with words from Exercises 1 and 2. The first letter is given to help you.

A recent vote on the Internet on the best piece of technology of the 20th century had no real surprises. The calculator, when it first appeared was
[1] e_____ and [2] u_____, saving the mathematical lives of many students in maths exams! Thirty years after this [3] d_____ first appeared, it has still not become [4] o_____ and is used by family accountants everywhere. In fact it is
[5] g_____ like the calculator that dominate the list. The digital watch was a [6] c_____ product when it first appeared. Now it seems [7] o_____.
However, it was still the third most popular on our list. The winner was the mobile phone. Although many people said a mobile phone, with an average life of 12 months, wasn't very [8] d_____, it is so
[9] h_____ for day to day life.

VOCABULARY: opposites

1a Write these words under the correct heading to show which prefix they use to make the opposite.

| like (vb)   effective   accurate   efficient |
| management   necessary   equality |
| likely   trust (n)   appropriate   able (adj) |
| convenient   sensitive |

in-	dis-	mis-	un-

1b Complete the sentences with words from above. Use the word or its opposite.

1 The cleaning company is so _____.
   They took six hours to finish when I could have done it in four.

2 The GPS system is very _____ at getting a signal anywhere, thanks to its satellite connection.

3 Their relationship was damaged by _____ after Jane lied to Helen.

4 I can make the six o'clock appointment but it's quite _____. I'll have to cancel my aerobics class.

5 The collapse of the Turtle Foundation is a classic story of _____, especially that of the CEO, Harold Mintzberg.

6 It would be _____ to say that I _____ technology. I just think life was simpler without it.

7 How could you be so _____!
   He's just lost his mother.

TRANSLATION

2 Translate the negative words in Exercise 1a into your language.

in-   dis-

1 _____   8 _____

2 _____   mis-

3 _____   9 _____

4 _____   10 _____

5 _____   un-

6 _____   11 _____

7 _____   12 _____

                                 13 _____

DICTATION

3a 2.27 Listen and write what you hear.

_____

_____

_____

_____

_____

_____

_____

_____

_____

3b Read what you have written. Tick the true statement.

1 A TV series is a bad example of life without technology.

2 People will find it easy to live without technology.

3 Without electricity there will still be technology.

4 The speaker conducted research on how people would survive without technology.

LISTENING

4 `2.28` Listen to what people said about the possibility of life without technology. Tick the correct box for each speaker.

Speaker	Likely	Not sure/ Does not say	Unlikely
1			
2			
3			
4			
5			
6			
7			
8			

5 `2.28` Listen again. Which speaker gives the following opinions?

a) People will remember how important the world around us is. ____

b) We won't be able to keep up to date with the news. ____

c) Humans will find it impossible to adapt. ____

d) People will have to learn about different ways of eating. ____

e) I hope it won't happen during my life. ____

f) Humans need to think about the limits of developing technology. ____

g) There will always be technology. ____

h) We are not being told everything. ____

GRAMMAR: conditionals (1)

6a Write sentences from the listening using the prompts below.

1 oil / run out / eventually find / source of power

_____

2 maybe / better / have to live / without technology

_____

3 imagine / have / no light at night / we / survive?

_____

4 technology / die / I think / millions / die

_____

5 have to rely / mail / we / out of date / news

_____

6 as long as / have / power / be / fine

_____

7 we / not create electricity / so many things / not work

_____

8 provided / rich / you / fine

_____

9 supposing / wake up / in dark / in middle of night / what / you / do?

_____

_____

6b `2.29` Listen and check.

6c Which of the sentences are first conditional and which are second conditional?

first conditional:

_____

_____

second conditional:

_____

_____

READING

1 Match sentences A–F with gaps 1–6.

A People always think 'It will never happen to me' when it comes to losing data.

B Less dramatic than e-rage perhaps, failure to take care of your computer is also an issue.

C The majority of mishaps involve laptop computers, which are easier to damage or lose.

D An argument that technophobes have used over the years has been that machines cannot replace humans and that machines cannot be trusted to function all the time.

E There is also an emerging trend in the different ways men and women handle their loss.

F There is no question that machines are becoming more and more advanced and less likely to crash or break down.

DATA LOSS:
HUMAN ERROR OR MACHINE ERROR?

1____ Recent evidence could suggest that while the technophobes are correct with the first half of their accusation, they may not be so correct with the rest. In fact, recent research suggests that in more and more cases it is the human being who is responsible for the failure of technology, particularly in the world of computers and, specifically with regard to the loss of data. Data recovery experts, the technological doctors and nurses of desktop or laptop hard drives, say the technical breakdown of computers is still the main cause of data loss, although human error in the form of lack of care and even rage is fast becoming one of the main reasons files need rescuing.

2____ However, it is clear that users still have to do more to protect their data. In fact, it may be true that precisely because computers have become less likely to break down, humans have been less careful with using the computer, and have become more responsible than the machines themselves for the loss of data. In fact this trust has become so strong that when a user feels 'betrayed' by his or her machine, they may react in extreme ways. For example, take the American man who was so frustrated with his laptop that he shot it in a fit of e-rage. Once he calmed down he realised that there were important files he needed. Amazingly the data recovery experts were able to retrieve them.

3____ One company director would not have lost his company's business accounts if his laptop hadn't accidentally fallen into the bath he was having. Another businessman lost all the notes for his presentation because he left his laptop on the roof before getting into the car and driving off.

4____ There are countless examples of people forgetting them on public transport and in cafés or bars. Experts recommend data be backed up daily or weekly and regular checks are made on back-up systems to ensure they are working, especially, in the case of laptops.

5____ More men than women seem to be likely to try and retrieve the data themselves before asking for help from the experts, which can sometimes lead to more damage to the computer. A user who had problems with his DVD drive actually tried to fix the computer with his trusted screwdriver, resulting in the computer refusing to work at all.

6____ However, the truth is that it could quite well happen to you. Although the user may have little control when the ghost in the machine causes the loss, they have a lot of control over what they do when they use their computers. Technology will always only be as good as the person using it, no matter how advanced the technology is … at least until technology finds its users obsolete.

READ BETTER

Many articles or academic texts include a mix of fact and speculation (guesses or things that may be true). It is important for the reader to be able to identify between what is accepted as true and what the writer believes may be true. The following words will suggest to the reader that the point being made is speculation:

the use of verbs such as *may, could, might, seem, believe, claim, hope, think, suspect, suggest*

the use of adverbs such as *possibly, probably, perhaps*

NOTE: We can only identify what is fact or speculation in the opinion of the author.

2 Read the article again. Tick the points which are just speculation.

1 Research showing humans are responsible for the failure of technology. ____

2 The technical breakdown of computers being the main cause of data loss. ____

3 Users becoming less careful because of the sophistication of computers. ____

4 Men being more likely to try to retrieve data. ____

5 Technology being only as good as the user. ____

GRAMMAR: conditionals (2)

3a Match examples A–C, form a–c and meanings 1–3.

Examples

A One company director would not have lost his company's business accounts if his laptop hadn't accidentally fallen into the bath he was having.

B If you hadn't shot your computer, we would have the estimates now.

C If you weren't so careless, you might not have left your laptop on the top of the car.

Form

a) *if* + past simple + *would/might/could* + *have* + past participle

b) *if* + past perfect + *would/should/might/could*, etc.

c) *if* + past perfect + *would/could/might* + *have* + past participle

Meaning

1 present condition with past result

2 unreal situation in the past

3 past condition with present result

3b Which of the sentences are third conditional and which are a mixed conditional?

third conditional:

_____

_____

mixed conditional:

_____

_____

4 Match the clauses to make conditional sentences.

1 If they hadn't lost the last game,

2 If we had met our targets,

3 We would be happier now

4 If it rained every year,

5 If they had added more sugar,

6 If we hadn't moved the satellite dish,

a) we would have had enough water last summer.

b) the chocolate might taste better.

c) they would have been champions.

d) we would have got a better connection.

e) we could have got a bonus.

f) if he had won the election.

5 Rewrite these sentences using third or mixed conditional.

1 We lost a lot of data because users are not careful enough.

If users *were more careful, we wouldn't have lost so much data*.

2 He shouldn't have used his screwdriver on his computer. It destroyed it.

If he _____.

3 No one wants the new watch since they increased the price.

If they _____.

4 You didn't come to the meeting so you couldn't vote.

If you _____.

5 People didn't hear about it so they are not frightened now.

If people _____.

6 Because it rained we can't cut the grass now.

If it _____.

KEY LANGUAGE: reassuring and encouraging

1a Complete the sentences with one or two words.

A My goodness! I can see how _____!

B Come on Dave, you can be frank with me and I promise you it won't go _____!

C Look, I _____ you feel, but we do believe in solving our problems here.

D Things'll get better, I _____.

E I can _____, we're going to put things right.

F Anyway, don't _____ Dave.

G Leave this with me and I _____ sort out the problems.

H Whatever happens, you won't be out of a job, you have _____ for that.

I Well that _____ very fair to me, I must say.

1b **2.30** Listen to the meeting and check. Put sentences A–I in the order you hear them.

1 ___ 4 ___ 7 ___
2 ___ 5 ___ 8 ___
3 ___ 6 ___ 9 ___

WRITING SKILLS: an article

1 Read the article. Tick the sentence which agrees with the main point that the writer is trying to give.

1 Large organisations used to spend a lot of money developing most new forms of technology.

2 The consumer is the person who is most responsible for the development of the less important forms of technology.

3 Thanks to state-run organisations, technology is developing very fast and in the right direction.

4 Because money is the main motivating factor, technology is not developing quickly enough in the right direction.

TECHNOLOGY: Driven By Demand

A Over the last hundred or so years [1] human beings have developed at an amazing rate. Who would have believed a hundred years ago that today we could receive messages from across the world in seconds? However, we might also ask if the people of a hundred years ago would have considered receiving messages as quickly as possible the most important need for society. (*Introductory topic sentence*)

B [2] Nobody denies that the computer is one of the most important pieces of technology today. It is important to note, however, that much of the development to improve computers is either in response to people's need to communicate on the Internet or to play games. [3] Why is this the case? The first thing to remember when trying to answer this question is that technology is developed and produced by private businesses and the main motivation of any private industry is most certainly the making of money. [4] There is no doubt, therefore, that these companies do not ask themselves whether their new device or machine will benefit society. [5] Rather they selfishly ask themselves whether the product will sell.

C Readers may see this as a positive development as it means that the consumer is the decision maker. Unfortunately, consumers are far more interested in [6] how to make their own little lives easier and less tedious than in developments that benefit the world. For example, [7] it is unquestionably true that an average teenager would prefer to read about the latest new computer game than the development of a fantastic little machine that removes bacteria from food. One supplies hours of fun for tired little minds, the other may save millions of people.

D It is also unfortunately the truth that such products as an anti-bacteria device are usually developed either by state-supported institutions or small organisations with little money. So, while these great projects struggle to find money, the big organisations can decide whether to design a game or a new entertainment system for their luxury fast cars.

E Why can't big companies use some of [8] their ridiculously large amounts of money and resources to support worthwhile developments? The bottom line is everything must make a profit.
[9] A machine to take bacteria out of food may be worthwhile but will housewives rush to buy it? Look at GPS systems. They were around for years before they started making money and why did they start making money? Because someone realised that they would be a nice luxury addition for their sports cars and marketed them that way.

F *(Concluding topic sentence)* __ Technology needs to focus on worthwhile projects which should then receive the money and attention they deserve. Until this happens, [10] for every character in a computer game that dies, more and more real people will follow.

WRITE BETTER

It is usually quite easy to identify the writer's opinions by focusing on the key ideas and topic sentences. When you write, to guarantee that your article or essay holds together, you should write an outline. An outline should include the main introductory sentence, the key points and the conclusion.

2 Match one introductory topic sentence (1–3) and one concluding topic sentence (4–6) with the gaps in the article.

Introductory topic sentences

1 The aim of this article is to argue that in fact we are more interested in providing technology that makes money than technology that actually helps us.

2 The aim of this article is to show that large organisations are controlling what we choose to buy and develop.

3 The aim of this article is to show that consumers have not developed to the point where they can be given the choice as to which technology we should develop.

Concluding topic sentences

4 In conclusion, organisations need to act more responsibly if they are to sell the technology they are developing.

5 In conclusion, it is totally unacceptable that the motivation for technology comes from big organisations and small people leading small lives.

6 In conclusion, if consumers took more time to find out about the world, they would understand how important it is to develop the right technology.

3 Tick which of the following topics are covered by paragraphs B–E.

1 Everything must make a profit

2 Motivation to develop technology

3 Why people play games

4 How a product becomes more successful

5 Consumers' opinion of technology

6 The consumer decides

7 Problems that worthwhile development has

8 Why big companies develop worthwhile technology

4 Look at the underlined phrases in the article. Label them A–E. Some phrases may fit more than one category.

A emphatic statement	B strong adverb
C strong adjective	D strong language/image
E rhetorical question	

1 ____   6 ____

2 ____   7 ____

3 ____   8 ____

4 ____   9 ____

5 ____   10 ____

AUDIOSCRIPTS

CD1
Lesson 1.2 Track 1.3

Today I'd like to talk about the subject of subtitling. Many people around the world base their views on British and American life on what they see in films. To help this process, the dialogue for British and American films is translated into many languages. For example, how can audiences around the world understand the comedy in *Bridget Jones*? Before the film is released, the dialogue is translated and usually turned into subtitles. The original soundtrack is left in place and the translation is printed at the bottom of the screen. The translator of subtitles faces a unique challenge that other translators, luckily, don't have to deal with. That is, the real words on the soundtrack are presented with the subtitles. This means that anyone who understands both languages can immediately spot the mistakes. And this is why some of the most famous mistakes in translations are found in film subtitles.

For example, in one famous film an actor says that his friend is so crazy that he wanted to build a Greyhound depot on the highway. Instead of checking with someone, the translator used only a dictionary. A dictionary won't tell you that as well as a greyhound being a type of dog used in races, it is also the name of a bus company in America. So instead of translating the text as 'He is so crazy he wants to build a bus depot on the highway', he translated it as 'He wants to build a race track for dogs on the highway'!

Comedy is really difficult to translate, particularly the British use of irony. When the woman arrives late and the man says 'You're early', English and American audiences will laugh. But if the translator just translates the words, the audience will miss the meaning completely. Sometimes in fact, when you hear people laughing at the wrong time in a subtitled film, they are laughing at the subtitles, not the film.

Instead of subtitling, another choice is dubbing. This means that audiences don't have to read and also comedy can be better understood. However, dubbing a film changes the film and its culture, so if you watch an Arabic dubbing of the film, you will hear things that make sense in an Arabic culture but would never have been said in the original film. For example, in the original film one speaker talks about snow; in the dubbing the speaker talks about rain. Also, in many cases the natural sounds of a film are lost when it is dubbed and the experience of realism is lost. So, dubbing or subtitles? It's a difficult decision. Now, what I'd …

Lesson 1.3 Track 1.4

O: So David … share with some of us 'old' people how language is changing.

D: Well, Ola, language is changing all the time but many of us don't realise it's happening or even wish it wouldn't happen.

O: Why's that?

D: Well, one reason is that many new words come from other languages. For example, the word 'bruschetta', or 'bruscetta' as people say, from Italian to describe a certain type of bread. In fact, many of these foreign words are related to food.

O: You mean like *kebab* and my favourite drink, a latte?

D: Yes, that's right. Many people don't like this. They don't think we should borrow words from other languages.

O: Hmm, seems strange to me. Why create a new word when a word that people recognise already exists?

D: Exactly. For example, many languages use the word 'television' – and it's easily recognisable. Another example is what we call portmanteau words.

O: Wow! What are they?

D: These are blended words created by putting two words together. For example, what do you call a teenager who spends all day on his computer?

O: A lazy boy?

D: Well, maybe. However, he will be better known as a 'screenager'. There are lots of other well-known examples such as 'brunch' – a combination of 'breakfast' and 'lunch'…

O: Of course – it's a meal many of us have at the weekend when we get up late – a great idea!

D: Yes, it is – it's usually eaten around 11.00 in the morning. OK, what about these ones which are very familiar today: *Bollywood* and *motel*?

O: Well, I know what Bollywood means – it's the Indian film industry – but I'm not sure what the two words are. One of them must be 'Hollywood', but what about the 'B'? Bengal? Big?

D: No, actually it's 'Bombay'.

O: Of course! And *motel* – well that's been in the English language for ages – I didn't even know it was made up of two words. It must be something to do with 'hotel', and the 'm' must be something like 'mini' or 'mobile'… oh, I know – they're always by the road, and you usually stay in them while driving somewhere, so it's probably 'motor' – 'motor hotel'?

D: Absolutely right. And there are lots of other examples. There are also what we call TLAs.

O: And what are those?

D: They are three-letter abbreviations. For example, B2B means 'business to business' and NIH means 'not invented here'.

O: But people don't actually say those things, do they?

D: Yes they do, unfortunately for us. For example, last week I heard someone say 'IMO it would be a good idea'.

O: IMO?

D: Yes, 'in my opinion'. This is becoming more and more common, especially when people write on the Internet or use their mobiles to communicate.

O: It seems it's becoming a whole new language! Now tell me, do you …

Lesson 1.4 Track 1.6

A: All right. So, we need to get the contract signed by the end of the day. I'm sure Claudio wants to sign and the club certainly wants him. I'm sure we can sort it out, but we don't have much time to do it.

B: The problem is that Claudio doesn't speak any English and he's not sure he can come and live in England alone.

A: Yes, I can see it's rather a difficult situation. Would language classes help?

B: Well, there's the problem. If Claudio attends intensive English classes, which he needs, he won't be able to train properly and without proper training he won't play well. If he doesn't play well, then the club loses. On the other hand, if he can't speak English, he'll be unhappy and won't play well and again the club loses. As you can see, it's a vicious circle for both Claudio and the club.

A: Hmm. It's a very tricky situation, isn't it? Does Claudio have a family?

B: Yes. He is very close to his brother, who speaks good English.

A: Good. I think the best way to deal with this is for the club to pay for Claudio's brother to come with him to England and live with him for the first year.

B: That might well solve the problem, but what will his brother do in England? He has a job back home.

A: The club could find him one, couldn't they?

B: The trouble with that is that if his brother is out working, Claudio won't see him during the day, when he will need his brother's help the most.

A: OK, then the club will pay him to be his brother's helper. It'll cost them more money but if Claudio is such a good player they'll think it's worth it. What do you think?

B: Yes, I think that seems to be the way forward but we'd better talk to Claudio and the club quickly.

AUDIOSCRIPTS

Lesson 1.5 Track 1.7

Good evening ladies and gentleman. In this talk I intend to discuss whether parents who come from different nationalities should teach their baby both languages or only one. First, I want to talk about how children learn languages. Then, I want to talk about the advantages of teaching children both languages at the same time. Next, I will talk about the disadvantages and finally, I will give my opinion on this issue.

Let's begin with how children learn. The most important thing to remember is that children do not learn their first language like they learn language in school. In other words, children at school learn by reading, writing and doing exercises. When a baby learns a language it cannot read or write. It can only learn by listening, passively memorising and then speaking. This means that it needs to hear the language as much as possible. For instance, a mother may need to say 'Mama' and 'Dada' twenty or thirty times a day for three or four months before her child begins to use these words to talk about his or her parents.

Lesson 2.3 Track 1.10

Peter Smith, Dr Aykut

P: Thank you for coming onto the show, Dr Aykut. To begin with, I'd like to know how many earthquakes Istanbul has had.

DR: Good afternoon Peter. Istanbul has had 15 heavy earthquakes in the last 1,500 years. It's probably had hundreds of other little ones too but let's say 15 to be clear.

P: That seems a lot to me, but what do I know? Could you tell me when the last earthquake in Istanbul was?

DR: The last big earthquake was in 1894. There is no record of how many people were killed but the damage was extensive. I think at least a few thousand people were killed.

P: That's very sad. Can I ask when the last big earthquake in Turkey was?

DR: That's a very good question. There are earthquakes in Turkey all the time but the last big one was in Izmit in 1999. In fact, there were two earthquakes.

P: Really? Could you tell me if the Izmit earthquake was close to Istanbul?

DR: It was very close indeed, about 80 kilometres from the city.

P: Hmmm. Do you know how many people were killed in the Izmit earthquake?

DR: We will never be completely sure. But the final official figure was 20,000 people. Many, many more people lost their homes.

P: That's terrible. Do you know whether the Izmit earthquake affected Istanbul?

DR: Yes it did. The shocks were felt in Istanbul. Some people died and there were some houses damaged. It is because of these earthquakes that people are now worrying about Istanbul.

P: Really? So, Dr Aykut, could you tell me if there is a strong possibility of an earthquake in Istanbul?

DR: This is the big question. There is always a big chance of an earthquake in Istanbul but, according to our research there is a 62% chance that there will be a major earthquake in Istanbul in the next 30 years.

P: Wow!

Lesson 2.3 Track 1.11

A: OK for the second part of the interview, what are we going to ask her?

B: How about 'How big is the chance of an earthquake in Istanbul?'

C: That was asked in the first part. Wake up, Joe!

A: Well, we should ask a question connected with that. OK, what about 'Why do you think an earthquake will happen soon?'

C: Yes, and we can follow it with, 'How big will the earthquake be?'

B: Yes, and then how about 'Why would an earthquake be bad for Istanbul?'

A: Don't be silly, Joe. Of course an earthquake is bad for Istanbul!

B: OK, OK, then change it to 'What will happen if there is a major earthquake in Istanbul?'

C: That's good.

A: Yes it is. Let's also have 'What do people need to do?' Then Dr Aykut can talk about preparations to protect Istanbul.

B: Yes and we can ask 'Is the government doing anything?'

C: OK. I read an article saying that some of the buildings are very dangerous in Istanbul. I'm sure Dr Aykut will want to talk about that.

B: Good. Let's ask 'Are there any problems with houses in Istanbul?'

A: How many questions have we got?

B: Six. We need two more. The obvious question is 'Should people be worried?'

C: That should be the last question. We haven't asked when. Let's ask 'Can you predict when the earthquake will be?'

A: Yes and that's enough. Well done everyone.

Lesson 2.4 Track 1.12

A: Let's talk about the government decision on alternative sources of power. It seems they won't agree to wave power.

B: I'd like to know how you discovered that. No one's been told yet.

A: A friend at a newspaper told me. They're going to announce their decision tomorrow. I believe they think it's too expensive.

D: You're absolutely right! They think it's too expensive and too slow.

B: What about solar power? It's certainly not as expensive as wave power.

A: You have a point, but don't you think the answer is too simple? I'm sure they have already thought about solar power.

B: Well, that's one way of looking at it but what else can they choose? There isn't another choice!

A: What about this new 'sugar power'? I read something in a report and I'm interested in knowing more about it. It's certainly something I know very little about.

D: I'd go along with you there. Peter Davis thinks it could be really useful.

B: Oh come on! It's useless!

C: For our purposes that's very true because it can only generate small amounts of electricity, I'm afraid.

A: Well then, what are we going to do?

Lesson 3.2 Track 1.14

Interviewer, Dr Smith, David Jones, Beverly Wilson

INT: Today we have invited several people to answer the question 'Is chess a sport?' Dr Smith, could you begin for us, please?

DR S: Of course. I believe chess is a sport. Many countries and sports organisations have now accepted that chess is a sport, for example the European Union, the Olympic Committee and even the British Government.

INT: OK, let's ask David Jones, a chess grandmaster.

DJ: Well, I'm sorry but what Dr Smith says is rubbish. Yes, some governments and organisations accept it's a sport but few people, including many chess players, do. It's a game, not a sport. Admittedly, it's a complex game, like Bridge and Go, but still, it's a game.

INT: Beverly Wilson, you're an MP in the British Government. What do you think?

BW: The government firmly believes it's a sport. Far too many sports are 'called' games and do not get the recognition they deserve, but we think it's time they did. For example, chess has its own established rules and competitions. There is a World Championship of Chess and chess will soon be played in the Olympics. Quite clearly, it's a sport.

DJ: Bridge also has a world championship, but it's a card game. Monopoly has a world championship too! Are you going to tell me Monopoly is a sport? Let me ask another question: how much physical activity is there in chess? I'll tell you – none, none at all!

DR S: That's not true! I agree there is little physical activity but, for example, players have to move the pieces.

DJ: But you can also play chess on a computer. Then there are no pieces ...

DR S: But then there is a mouse ...

DJ: Oh come on! Alright, there is hardly any physical activity in chess so it can't be a sport. The only reason chess is now a sport is so that it can receive money from the government ...

Lesson 3.4 Track 1.15

Sue, Peter, Dave

S: Right, so we have to have an article in next month's issue on one of the greatest moments in athletics. Peter, you have two suggestions.

P: That's right Sue. I gave you two small news reports to consider. What do you think?

S: Well, Roger Bannister's achievement is tremendous. It's undoubtedly one of the greatest moments in athletics history.

D: Well I'm not sure, Sue. Did you know that, for example, John Landy broke Bannister's record just 46 days later? That's just as incredible as Roger's.

S: Hmm, I don't know. We are interested in the moment, not the person. Maybe Landy was just as amazing a runner as Roger, but it was Roger who broke the barrier on that incredible day.

P: Yes it was. Just imagine it. That moment when he crossed the line and people stopped their watches must have truly been an important moment in athletics history.

S: Yes. But what about this other report? Winning a gold medal and breaking an Olympic record is impressive but not exactly original is it!

P: That's because that's not the end of the story. Within two weeks Emil Zatopek had won not only the 10,000 metres but also the 5,000 metres

and then, even more incredibly, the marathon too! That's over 35,000 metres in total!

D: Wow. Surely that's impossible.

S: Obviously not. And he was thirty years old, too. I think that's the one we'll go for. Peter, I want you to present the idea to the editor, OK?

P: Sure.

Lesson 3.4 Track 1.16

For our article next month, we've decided to go with Emil Zatopek. That he was a tremendous athlete is certain. There's no doubt about that. However, there is one competition that particularly shows Emil to undoubtedly be one of the greatest athletes in history. That was the 1952 Olympics in Helsinki. By the time of the marathon, Emil had already won the 10,000 metres and 5,000 metres and in both events he broke Olympic records. Any great athlete would have been totally exhausted by then, but not Emil. What's extraordinary, also, about Emil is that he had never run a marathon before the Olympics. But he didn't only win the marathon. What was really impressive was that he won it easily and again broke the Olympic record.

At a time when it was difficult to follow the whole race, imagine the faces of the spectators when Emil ran into the stadium to complete the marathon. Everyone in the stadium must have known they were watching an extraordinary moment in athletics history. But, most of all, since 1952 no one has repeated Emil's achievement.

Lesson 4.2 Track 1.18

A: Right everyone, we've been given the go-ahead to fly out to Italy tomorrow. The whole team is being put on the project to find a cure for this Chikungunya disease. So, here's the plan. We're meeting this evening at 7.00 to arrange the teams.

At that meeting we will be deciding who goes to Italy and who stays in the laboratory. There are going to be two teams on the plane to Italy tomorrow morning. Once we are there, one team will be trying to collect mosquitoes to bring back to the lab. We hope they will also be collecting blood samples from sufferers of the disease for testing. The second team will be trying out some of the experimental vaccines we've been working on. That team needs to evaluate the success of a vaccine and whether it would be more effective if it was used with boosters. Paul, what will your team be doing in the lab?

B: Well, until the other two teams fly back, we won't really be doing anything at all. Seriously, we're going to run a few extra tests on the experimental vaccines while the teams are in Italy. Maybe we can get something ready for you to take back. Once the teams get back, the fun really begins. We will be working night and day to find some new test vaccines.

A: OK. We have to do this fast. We are presenting this to the board at 8.30 a.m. Tuesday morning. We need something positive to show. Sarah, you are going to be responsible for supplies. Make sure we've got proper protection. The last thing I want is someone in the team picking up the disease. Which reminds me, we are going to need some mosquito specialists ...

Lesson 4.5 Track 1.22

All right, here's my report on St Swithin's hospital website. I used the website, the links it offers and the opinions of people who used the site to conduct my investigation. OK, so what did I discover? First of all, it's not clear what the purpose of the website is. There is a section of useful telephone numbers and a 'contact us' section. There is also news about the hospital. However, there are also articles by some of the doctors and surgeons and there is also a useful links section which seems to mostly lead people to places to buy things online. So what is it? Is it a resource for patients and friends and family of patients? Is it a window for doctors and surgeons to publish articles, or is it a link to Internet shopping? The next thing I discovered was that it was last updated six months ago. This undoubtedly meant that all the hospital news was pretty useless.

Thirdly, I checked the list of people working at the hospital and there are some reputable and well-known doctors and surgeons there. However, this is not mentioned on the website. The articles were mostly written by people I have never heard of. Finally, I discovered that the website was set up and looked after by two of the doctors at the hospital. I also discovered that one of these doctors has just left the hospital.

To sum up this is a very poor website indeed and something needs to be done quickly. It is a good idea for the hospital to hire a professional company to recreate the website and it is vital that the hospital prepares a clear description of what they want on the website. Finally, the hospital must understand that the old website cannot continue and therefore it must be removed immediately.

AUDIOSCRIPTS

Lesson 5.3 Track 1.24

PART ONE

In this presentation I'd like to talk about my favourite attempt to bring literature to TV. It is not a normal case however. In 1873, Jules Verne wrote the great novel *Around the World in Eighty Days*, where an English gentleman succeeded in travelling round the world using the most modern forms of transport available at the time. He managed to complete his journey with minutes to spare.

In 1988, Michael Palin, a well-known actor and comedian attempted to do the same thing. Of course, it would've been easy if he had used planes and fast cars to do it. However, Michael had to use the same means of transport that would have been available to Jules Verne's character, Phileas Fogg, in 1873. This meant Michael wasn't allowed to use planes and cars but had to use trains and ships instead. The journey was recorded for TV and shown in 1989.

Lesson 5.3 Track 1.25

PART TWO

As I have said, Palin wasn't able to use modern forms of transport, but could use any form of transport that was available to Phileas Fogg, whether or not he actually used it. Palin started on the Orient Express and didn't have to get off until he was in Austria, when he was unexpectedly held up by a strike by railway workers. He managed to get out of Austria by coach, and I mean horse-drawn coach here, not a bus coach. He took the coach into Greece and then was able to take a boat across to Egypt. In Egypt, however, he had a lot of trouble. First of all, he had difficulty finding a train to Cairo and then, once he got there, he found out that his boat was damaged and could not leave. This meant that he couldn't make his connection to Saudi Arabia. Although, according to the rules of the bet, Palin wasn't allowed to use a car, it was decided to allow Palin to drive to Saudi Arabia to save the trip. Thankfully he didn't have to 'cheat' again. By the time Palin reached Bombay he was a week behind Phileas Fogg. Again, in India, Palin had ship problems but he managed not to lose any more time. Of course, by the time Palin was travelling around the world, ships were faster and safer. This meant that Palin was able to make up all the lost time by the time he reached the US.

Although balloons are associated with Phileas Fogg, he never actually used one in *Around the World in Eighty Days*. However, Palin was able to experience balloon travel and also being pulled by dogs on a sled, as he travelled across the US. Palin arrived back in London 17 hours ahead of schedule. In the TV series we experienced all the variety and excitement of travelling across the world whilst trying to keep to a deadline. It also showed how difficult it must have been for Phileas Fogg to win his bet. For this reason I think this series was a great way of bringing the novel to life on TV.

Lesson 5.4 Track 1.28

Murat and Janosz

M: There's no doubt in my mind, Janosz that the tests have been a failure. The car still isn't ready to drive. I think the answer is to postpone tests and go back to the laboratory.

J: I'm not so sure, Murat. Don't you think that the brakes have improved in testing? They were much worse in earlier tests.

M: Yes, that's true. But surely you can't argue that it's ready to go on the road? The test dummy went straight through the window!

J: But you must agree that wasn't our fault! David forgot to put the seat belt on the dummy!

M: Did he? I didn't know. But I'm sure you can see that we can only put this car on the market when we are sure it's safe. Can you really say it's safe right now?

J: To be honest, no. But I really think that we've made some progress. Remember how hopeless we felt last week? Testing is the key. It's the way forward for us.

M: Yes. We have made progress. Yet, it's essential to remember our responsibility to the drivers of our cars. They must feel safe. OK, I think the best solution would be to spend another week on safety tests and then decide.

J: I agree. That's the best way to go for now.

Lesson 6.3 Track 1.30

Let's begin with me giving you an introduction to some of the writing habits of great writers. These habits can be divided into two types. Firstly, those types related to writing style, and secondly, those referring to writing environment. And as we do this, we're going to talk about some of the greatest writers in world literature. So, let's start with Ernest Hemingway. Did you know that Hemingway used to write exactly 500 words a day? That's right. Not one word more, not one word less. Why did he do this? Well, that's a question we could ask of many writers and only receive the answer 'Because it worked for me'. What we need to remember is that writers are a superstitious lot! Hemingway honestly believed that if he wrote more or less than 500 words his books would be a failure. This is certainly not a habit I suggest you follow. The number of words doesn't matter. You will understand this more when you have a white piece of paper in front of you and you are desperate for *any* word!

A similar writer was Anthony Trollope. He would only write from five thirty until eight thirty every morning and would try to write 250 words every 15 minutes. This means that he was an incredibly fast writer. If you can do this, it will also mean that you will be very popular with your publisher! Unlike Hemingway, Trollope's habit makes some sense. As dreams have often been a very good source for the ideas we write about, it makes some sense to write as soon as we wake up. Secondly, we are usually more clear-minded first thing in the morning and so we can concentrate better.

What about the context to write in? Balzac used to need to drink at least ten espressos a day to be able to write. While I don't suggest you drink that much, coffee has often been called the fuel that drives writers. Personally, I only need water but there you go. Proust used to feel more comfortable writing in bed. Again, there is some logic to this. We need to feel relaxed if we want to write well. On the other hand, Thomas Wolfe would have to be standing up before he could write. This need suggests that Wolfe had concentration problems or perhaps he was afraid of being too lazy.

As you can see, most writers had good reasons for their habits. However, as Somerset Maugham once said, 'There are three rules for writing a novel. Unfortunately, no one knows what they are.' Writing is about you finding out what suits you best, so don't expect to be told how to write. Expect to discover for yourself. Now, if we can start with the first task I have for you today …

Lesson 6.4 Track 1.33

Tom, Mary

M: Well Tom, we've all heard about the Keitai phenomenon in Japan and how it's changed the writing world there. We're hoping that this new technology you're developing will have a similar impact here in the UK. If all goes well, we hope to have the first new phones out by December.

T: That's great Mary. We've been very happy to work with you before and think this is another great opportunity for cooperation. As you know, in the past we have always agreed on 15 percent of the profit, but in this case, we think 25 percent is more appropriate. This is revolutionary technology which will change how

AUDIOSCRIPTS

people use their mobiles, and we feel that if you agreed with us on the deal, you'd be guaranteed to make a huge profit.

M: Twenty-five percent you say?

T: You'll find it's very good value for money.

M: Really, we weren't expecting to pay as much as that. It's going to be a hard sell – as you know we rely on our investors and they were actually hoping to agree on 10 percent. If you included the other program we talked about, it'd make it more attractive for us.

T: Unfortunately I don't know if we can do that. How about if I talked to our development team and got back to you on that?

M: That's fine but that leaves me with nothing to go back to the investors with.

T: Look. I'd like to make a proposal. Let's start with 15 percent and we'll raise it to 25 percent after the first six months.

M: Sounds good to me but I still have to think what the investors will say.

T: Why don't you show the product to your investors? I think they'll love it!

M: We'll do that. Meanwhile, we need time to think about this, and take some advice.

T: Could I suggest we meet again next week?

M: I think we'll need a little longer than that. Let's say two weeks today.

T: All right then, but the longer we can't reach an agreement, the more likely it is that we will need to look elsewhere.

CD2
Lesson 7.3 Track 2.3

Speaker A
In my opinion the best site or sites in Warsaw are the Warsaw Uprising Monuments. There is one really thrilling monument where a moment from history is captured – like a picture was taken as soldiers were being helped underground to escape from the guns. There is another one which shows a little child with a gun and boots that are much too big for him. Every time I see it I want to cry. On the other hand, the Old Town doesn't have any atmosphere at all. People forget that the Old Town was built recently. It looks like an old painting, and like a painting, it has no soul.

Speaker B
I hate the Palace of Science and Culture. It's so ugly. It's not even Polish. When it was being built, most Polish people took no notice of it. I think that's why they made it so tall! For me, the best part of Warsaw is Nowy Swiat or New World Street. Here you can do your shopping

and buy the most modern things, in a street that looks like the 1930s. You could almost be in Paris.

Speaker C
I know most people won't agree, but for me the Palace of Science and Culture is a symbol of Warsaw. I know it has been given a bad name by people but it has watched all the changes in Warsaw over the last fifty years. Think about all the new buildings that were being demolished and rebuilt at that time, and yet it remained. I bet it would have a very interesting story to tell! However, I don't like the monuments of the Warsaw Uprising. I think they are too dramatic and also there are too many of them. Yes, I agree some of them are great but we must be careful not to overdo it. There's another to be built in Rembertow next month!

Speaker D
The Old Town is a great achievement. Imagine! A whole area was completely destroyed and then rebuilt in less than 20 years. I love walking through the streets of the Old Town. I know that the buildings haven't been there for a long time but they help us get an idea of what it was like. I don't like the Palace of Science and Culture. I have been told that it's not really Polish but that doesn't matter. It's just not very nice. It's just like a fat needle. Also, it doesn't really fit with the rest of the city. Warsaw has been planned in a way that brings the past and the future together. The style of the Palace of Science and Culture just doesn't look like part of Poland's past or future.

Lesson 7.4 Track 2.4

A: So let's start with the first-year courses. Do you think we can offer the same as last year?

B: Of course. I think it's absolutely essential to offer the *Introduction to Architecture* course. As we've discovered in the past, students know hardly anything about the subject before they come here. Usually the only thing they've ever done is look at some buildings and read some magazines!

A: I agree. But is that enough? Yes, we can offer *Introduction to Architecture* but I think we should also offer a *History of Architecture* course. If we can get them to start recognising classical designs early, it will make life a lot easier later.

B: Hmmm. All right. I see your point. I've always felt leaving it until the third year was a bit late. However, I'm sorry to be a bit practical, but we'd have to find out first if there were any books in the bookshop. I mean ones which are easy to follow for first-year students.

A: So we've got to get in touch with the bookshop pretty quickly. OK. I'll deal with that as I'll probably be teaching the course.

B: Let's look at the second year. We've got Dr Ervani here this year and it's vital we have him do a high profile course. It will be good not only for the students but for the university as a whole. Even our teachers might learn something!

A: Yes …, you're right, but we need to think this through. Dr Ervani is a very important and influential man and he's also quite a difficult person to work with. I'm not sure he'd be too happy working with second-year students. It might be a good idea to have him teach the fourth year students.

B: Oh come on, Mike! Most of our fourth-year students are already spending most of their time out of the university. It would be a huge waste of Dr Ervani's talents.

A: But it will be an easy job, which I think is exactly what Dr Ervani wants. Remember Paula, we certainly need his knowledge. However, we also need to keep him happy otherwise the Rector will be furious.

Lesson 8.1 Track 2.7

1 multinational <u>companies</u>
2 fair <u>trade</u>
3 consumer <u>choice</u>
4 natural re<u>sour</u>ces
5 human <u>rights</u>
6 child <u>labour</u>
7 <u>cli</u>mate change
8 global <u>warming</u>
9 corporate <u>greed</u>
10 free <u>markets</u>

Lesson 8.3 Track 2.9

Presenter, Mike, Anne

P: OK, over the last few weeks we've been looking at role models in different areas of society. Today we're going to look at role models in business, particularly a role model for outsourcing. In business today, we live in a world of outsourcing. What does this mean? Let's talk to Mike Hartley, owner of Hartley Marketing. So, Mike, what do you do?

M: Well, in-company what we do is we meet people who want to have their product advertised. We meet with them and agree on possible ideas.

P: And then you prepare the advertising?

M: Er, no. We contract other companies to do the work for us.

P: What do you mean?

92 AUDIOSCRIPTS

M: Well, last month, for example, a company (I won't mention who they are or the name of their product) wanted to have some colour posters done for their new product. So, we had the designs prepared by a design company, we had the posters printed by a printing company and we had everything boxed by a packaging company.

P: So what were you doing? Sitting in the office and having coffee?

M: No, I was having my hair done. No, I'm joking. I discovered early on in this business that you have to look after the customer and make sure they get exactly what they want. If I am spending all my time doing everything, I can't concentrate enough on the quality. By outsourcing all the work, I can spend the time checking everything, being the communication link between the customer and the designer and making sure everyone stays happy. To this date I've never had a call from a customer saying that they've had their campaign ruined by our poor posters or brochures. With time on my hands I can assure quality.

P: So then you turn up at the customer at the end of the process with a product that you didn't make.

M: No way! Every Monday we have all our stuff collected by a delivery service. So we let them deliver it. Listen, we are often running about eight projects at the same time so I can't do the delivery myself. I don't have the time.

P: Thanks, Mike. We also have Dr Anne Spencer from Warwick University here. Dr Spencer, what do you think of Mike? Is he a role model for business?

A: Well I'm not sure you can have a role model for business. Anyway, everyone talks about outsourcing but it does have disadvantages and it does have to be done for a good reason. Mike's definitely got the right idea, but if making sure you spend time with the customer is the key, then I wonder why Mike doesn't deliver himself. For example, if the company phones up and says 'Sorry, but we've had the wrong posters delivered', what's he going to do? Secondly, when something is done in-house, it's easy to keep to deadlines. However, I'm sure the designers and the packagers have other projects too. What if they phone you and say 'Sorry, we've had to move the date of printing as we haven't finished something else'? I'd be interested to know what Mr Hartley would do then.

M: Well, I think …

Lesson 8.4 Track 2.11

A: I think it's all about personality.

B: What do you mean by that?

A: OK. What I really wanted to say was it is the personality of a person that is mainly responsible for role modelling.

B: Sorry, I don't know what you mean.

A: Don't you? Hmm. Let me rephrase that then. To become a role model you need to have a certain type of personality.

B: Could you give me a specific example?

A: Of course. Think about a pop star. What sort of personality do they need? Well, they have to be ambitious and they have to be outgoing to begin with. Basically, what I'm saying is that if you haven't got the right personality, you're unlikely to be a role model. A quiet, shy person is not a role model for a pop star.

Lesson 9.2 Track 2.13

Cassandra, John

C: 628646?

J: Hello, is that Cassandra Morley?

C: Yes.

J: Hi, this is John Thatcher – the photographer. We arranged to talk about your photoshoot?

C: Oh yes! Hi John. Well, er, what can you tell me?

J: Well, first of all you didn't mention if you were doing it alone or not. Make sure you have a few assistants/helpers to provide the extra hands you'll find you need. Things could go wrong and you'll need the help.

C: There's a few of us going so that shouldn't be a problem.

J: All right. The first thing I suggest you do is write up a list of important things, for example, time and place, purpose of shooting, equipment you need and props, the things you may use in the pictures. Then make sure everyone has a copy of that list.

C: That's a good idea. It makes sure we don't forget anything.

J: As you're outside, have you thought about the weather? Make sure you get a weather forecast and know what to do if the weather gets bad. You could end up freezing and starving in the middle of nowhere.

C: OK … Yes, got that.

J: Have you thought about lighting?

C: For example?

J: Well, did you know that photography is Latin and means 'painting with light'? You need to think about how you're going to light the image, and what that light will look like. I suggest bringing along lights, reflectors, and people to set them up, hold them, move them, etc. Without them the results could be really terrible.

C: I like that about painting with light. Photography is a fascinating medium, isn't it!

J: Yes, it is. Right, what about the house? Have you actually seen it? There might be people living in it. If it's derelict, it could be quite dangerous.

C: No, I've been up there … and considering what we're doing it won't be a problem.

J: OK. What about the filming itself? Make sure you control the environment. You want to make sure nothing unexpected happens in your pictures.

C: OK … although something unexpected might make things look better …

J: No, you misunderstand me. In a big shoot last year I didn't control the environment properly and the images came out completely wrong. Take as many pictures as you can of the same image as you may lose some frames and the ones you do get may be utterly impossible to use.

C: Yes, that's excellent advice.

J: What else? Ah yes, do you know the models?

C: What models?

J: Well, you're going to need models for a photoshoot.

C: Ah, no. No, I'm not a photographer as such. I'm an artist and we're doing an artistic scene.

J: I'm sorry …

C: Yes, we're going to demolish the house using hammers and wearing business suits to show the destructive power of big business. I'm going to use a digital camera to take the pictures and …

J: I'm sorry you've got the wrong person. Talk to someone in your department who knows more about the art you're interested in, not a professional photographer. Goodbye.

C: … hello…. hello

Lesson 9.4 Track 2.15

All right, Steve has asked me to talk about Dr Salgado, who I met last week. First, I'll give you some basic facts about his life and academic background. Finally, I'll describe my opinion of him as a person.

OK, well Dr Salgado was born in Sri Lanka but was educated in the UK. He finished school with six GCSEs and then went to technical college to study architecture. From there he went on to study Modern Art at Oxford. This may be a strange path to take, but he had already started writing about art on the Internet and he was making a name for himself. When he finished his degree he then did a doctorate in alternative art, specialising in BritArt and the Tattoo Culture.

Right, I've told you a bit about his education. So moving on now to his career, it's actually rather short as he only finished his doctorate two years ago. During that time he was an assistant. After finishing his doctorate he left the University and spent two years as a critic on the Internet. He also set up the now famous Art Department at the Net University and gave live lectures on the Internet. Right, now you know a bit about his career, except to say that Dr Salgado is already a popular, if not controversial, art critic, especially with the sort of people we want to attract to the university. OK, that's it for his background.

Let's go on to how I found him … er, his personality. Well, he is really sure of himself and confident. He speaks well and knows his modern art and has a keen understanding of alternative art. However, he is quite ignorant of classical art and seems to be more interested in art as a business rather than art as a topic. He gets quite aggressive when questioned on this.

To sum up I think it would be good for the university to have him in the department but I think we will have trouble with other members of staff and I think we shouldn't let him anywhere near our first and second years. OK, that's all I have to say about Dr Salgado.

Lesson 10.3 Track 2.18

Present, Dr Sarah Elfman

P: We're lucky to have with us tonight Dr Sarah Elfman, who is lecturer in Psychology from Tilberg University and Director of Management Profilers UK, to take part in our question and answer session on 'Lying – Good or Bad?' In a few minutes I'll be asking students to put their questions to Dr Elfman, but first of all, Dr Elfman, in your opinion, is it possible to tell when someone is lying?

DR E: Well, most people would immediately answer 'Yes'. People really believe that liars show physical characteristics to prove they are lying. For example, liars don't look at you when they lie.

P: Is there any evidence of this?

DR E: Of what people think? Yes. The majority of people asked by scientists 'How can you tell when people are lying', insisted that liars avoid looking at you.

P: And is this true?

DR E: It is as true as liars growing long noses when they lie, just like Pinocchio. In fact, there is also no truth in the belief that liars can't sit still when they lie, or that they touch their noses. The result emerging from detailed research into the behaviour of lying is that, in fact, there is no physical reaction to help the listener deduce that the speaker is lying.

P: How does this affect your work as a Management Profiler?

DR E: Well this is very interesting. The first issue we have to consider is 'What is a lie?' For example is it a lie if you try and convince someone that the product you're selling is the best on the market, knowing full well that it isn't? Is it a lie if you tell one of your staff that their job is safe after being confidentially told by the manager that 500 people will be made redundant by December? I think it is very difficult to separate lies from different levels of truth so this question is difficult to answer. However, if you do argue that all of these are lies, then it's not hard to see that the ability to lie is a skill highly valued by many businesses.

P: But is it a skill Dr Elfman, if it is impossible to know when someone is lying or not?

DR E: Well, that's an interesting question. I think that while it is true that the art of good lying can be learnt, it's difficult to describe what liars do as a skill. As I said, there is no physical reaction that is unique to liars. There are things we can say that are common to liars, though not necessarily unique.

P: And what are those?

DR E: Well, even liars trained to be persuasive tend to overdo it. What I mean is their stories can be seen to be too good to be true. They make fewer errors in speech and rarely correct information or correct details as they speak. This is because they have already planned what they are going to say before they say it. Some companies today actually train their salespeople to hide their prepared speech by adding mistakes and pauses. It also seems to be the case that liars use a lot more body language. So, in conclusion, if someone is able to control these things then, yes, it could be said they have a skill.

However, let me state that not all liars display these signals and you cannot be sure someone is lying because they don't correct things they have said.

P: Thank you, Dr Elfman. Now, let me open the floor to …

Lesson 10.4 Track 2.20

Dr Elfman, Mr Gray

DR E: Well, you're right Mr Gray, you do have a problem in the Marketing Department. There are serious personality clashes and some very unhappy people.

G: As we feared, Dr Elfman. So what can we do about it? We don't want to sack anyone, but the Marketing Department just isn't working properly.

DR E: Well, if I were you, the first thing that I would do is change the Marketing Manager. He really doesn't have the personnel skills. It's essential that a Marketing Manager is respected by the team. But at the moment, the marketing team spend half the time talking behind his back. You might consider moving him into Sales. That would suit his personality much better.

G: All right, I'll look into that. However, that leaves me without a Marketing Manager.

DR E: Absolutely not, there's one staring you right in the face: Melanie Thatcher. She's highly respected by the team, hard-working and very approachable. She exhibits all the skills you need for the job. I think you need to talk to her about it first. I'm not sure she thinks she's ready yet. But, on the whole, I think she'd be perfect.

G: Really? I'd never have thought of Melanie. I'll have a chat with her tomorrow. However, it might be a good idea to keep it confidential. At least, until we know her position and announce the changes.

DR E: That's up to you, but believe me, it's vital that you make the changes soon before you start having people resign. Why don't you talk to Bill first? Get him in the right mood for a change to Sales. After all, if he gets defensive, you may have to take stronger measures which may take some time. You could also offer him some time away from the office. That will give him time to think about his future. But I would also advise you to be careful when you talk to him. He can be quite aggressive.

G: Hmm, I need to think about that.

AUDIOSCRIPTS

Lesson 10.4 Track 2.21

1 It's <u>essential</u> that a Marketing Manager is respected.

2 You <u>might</u> consider moving him into Sales.

3 I would <u>also</u> advise you to be careful.

4 I <u>think</u> you need to talk to her about it first.

5 It <u>might</u> be a good idea to keep it confidential.

6 It's <u>vital</u> that you make the changes soon.

Lesson 11.2 Track 2.23

Presenter, Abdul, Eman, Radhi

P: To talk to us a little bit about English Yemeni life I've invited along Abdul Qasem from Sheffield, his sister, Eman and his father, Radhi. Abdul, I understand your father came here in the fifties on his own to work in the steel industry. How did you feel when you received cards and photos of his life in England?

A: You thought, 'It must be heaven, all that greenery.' I'd never seen so many trees. It was fascinating.

P: Eman, how did you feel?

E: I started to forget what he looked like. When he came back, I opened the door for him and asked him who he was. When he told me he was my dad, he hugged me and I was really shy, because for a long time we'd been apart and I was thinking: 'Who is this guy?'

P: And when you finally came to England, Abdul, how did you feel?

A: It was how I expected – only better. It was a dream to join my dad here. However, I didn't know the whole story. In the fifties and sixties, people thought they were coming to a new, better life. But in many ways it turned out to be a life of hard work with little reward. You can't imagine some of the difficulties some had. Their whole life was their work to make money to send home. It's hard to believe but they sometimes wanted to minimise their spare time. The attitude was: You should never say no. And they couldn't afford to have a comfortable life. You hear from the older men about how overcrowded it could be, people sleeping under beds and sharing beds.

P: Radhi, you went back to Yemen when you retired. Were you disappointed about your life in England?

R: Not at all, no. I came back again this year because I felt I belonged here. Although I have a large family in Yemen, they want to stay there, but I want to stay here. I have become part of the community here.

A: Our community association runs an advice centre to help with cultural problems. They are also organising language classes. But some people find it difficult to resolve their cultural identity. One man who went back to Yemen said that he felt like a foreigner in his own country.

P: Tim Smith, who took the photos on display in the Coal, Frankincense and Myrrh exhibition, recently travelled to Yemen. Eman, I believe he talked to you about that experience?

E: Yes, that's right. He was introduced to people from Sheffield, Manchester and Cardiff. Some had worked in Britain and gone back, some were on holiday and some were people born in the UK of Yemeni parents. They were very surprised. Some of them hadn't spoken English or seen a white person for 30 years. He mentioned the town of Underfield to one man, and this man asked him if he knew it, grabbed his arm and just burst into tears.

P: Your husband is English – has he been to Yemen with you?

E: We're hoping to go next year – I know he'll love it. I'm planning to take my family there little things from England. Things that they miss like digestive biscuits and baked beans!

Lesson 11.3 Track 2.25

Guy, Susan

S: Listen Guy, we don't need to do the questionnaire, we can do a report without doing the questionnaire.

G: What do you mean?

S: Well we already know people who fit into the categories. For example, what about Karl? We keep inviting him to come out with us, like last week. What did he say?

G: He refused to come. Said he's saving money to buy a new house … that's long-term orientation, isn't it?

S: Yep and what about Yasmin? She has that boring job in town. She was offered a much better job but decided to stay at her old job because she felt safe.

G: That would mean … she's showing high uncertainty avoidance. OK, there's also Rowena. She admitted buying a Ferrari just because Marie Ansley bought a new car the week before.

S: That's right, so that's … masculinity. I don't think Rowena would be pleased to hear that! How about poor Anna? One minute she was doing well at uni and then suddenly she left to look after her grandmother.

G: I bet her parents persuaded her to leave.

S: No, not at all, she wanted to. That's a really good example of collectivism.

G: Hmm, I'm not so sure. OK then, there's those Swedish students who complained about their Japanese group leader making all the decisions without talking to them first. That's small power distance.

S: What? The Japanese student?

G: No, the Swedish ones. Hey, we're doing well here …

Lesson 11.4 Track 2.26

Good evening, everyone. I'd like to talk to you about the dangers of cultural loss. Culture represents the identity, traditions and art of a group of people, whether it is a nation or a small community. However, when one language and its culture begins to dominate, then other cultures are in danger.

The presentation is divided into three sections. I'll begin with the meaning of culture. I'll talk about why it is endangered and finally, I'll suggest things we can do to protect cultures.

OK, so what do we know about culture? Well … (*fade*)

… Turning now to the next part, why are cultures in danger? Well, the main reason is … (*fade*)

… and as one culture becomes more influential, it becomes harder and harder to convince younger people to keep to their culture. For example, it can be said that fast food has become popular and replaced traditional food in many cultures because of its association with American culture.

Let's now look at what we can do to protect local cultures from more dominant cultures. Is there anything that people can do? Well, yes there is … (*fade*)

… So, in conclusion, culture is important to people as it describes where they come from, who they are and where they are going to. Thanks to the work of cultural organisations around the world more and more cultures are being protected and the freer movement of people around the world has made cultural understanding easier and easier. Can more be done? I think so. What I think is needed is more cultural support in the home, at school and on the streets so that all people, especially young people, feel more pride in their own culture.

AUDIOSCRIPTS

Lesson 12.2 Track 2.28

Speaker 1
I don't know. If oil runs out, we'll eventually find another source of power. Human beings are too clever to stay in the dark for too long! My worry is that we don't know when to stop developing technology. Maybe it would be better if we had to live without technology.

Speaker 2
I think this will happen one day. It would be a disaster. Imagine if we had no light at night, how would we survive? Without light we'll end up cutting down all the trees to make fires. If technology died, I think millions of people would die too. Humans are not very good at adapting to a poorer standard of life.

Speaker 3
I'm a technophobe so I think it would be a good thing. A period of time without technology would force us to think again about what we have and what we don't have. We'll understand how unnecessary technology is to quality of life and it will highlight how insensitive we've been to the world around us. I know that technology will return in another form, so it won't die completely, but hopefully by then we will have realised that we need to be more careful with it.

Speaker 4
It's inaccurate to say we will lose technology. That's not possible. We'll just replace one type of technology with another. After a period of darkness we will adapt technologies or find basic technologies and start again. Nothing can stop the human race because we are always moving forward.

Speaker 5
Oh my goodness! I couldn't live without my computer. I have friends and family all over the world. How could I stay in touch with them? There'd be no phones either! My parents talk of contacting each other by post as recently as twenty years ago but that's no good. If we had to rely on mail, we would be so out of date with the news. The post is so inefficient. Could it happen? Who knows but I hope not!

Speaker 6
As long as we have power, we will be fine. Electricity in particular. If we cannot create electricity, then *so* many things will not work, like water heaters and air conditioners. It won't matter if you live in a hot or a cold place. Things will get bad very quickly wherever you are. I don't know what the result of this will be but I really hope I am not around to see it! I'm sure it will happen, though.

Speaker 7
I really believe that the government knows more than they are telling us. I'm certain that they have already prepared for such a situation. Of course we won't all benefit from these preparations if a disaster does happen. Provided that you're rich, you'll be fine. Disasters are not going to remove the inequality that exists in this world.

Speaker 8
Oh! That's a horrible thought. Supposing you woke up in the dark in the middle of the night, what would you do? There's no light to switch on! I'd be so frightened. We would have to learn to be self-sufficient but I'm not sure I'd be any good at that. Personally, I couldn't kill an animal for meat, I'm sure, but I don't know if you could be a vegetarian without technology. How would you make vegeburgers?

Lesson 12.4 Track 2.30

Dave, Mr Lloyd

D: Er, excuse me Mr Lloyd, could I have a word, please?

MR L: Of course Dave, come in … now, what can I do for you?

D: Well, I thought you should know that I'm thinking of resigning.

MR L: Wow, Dave. That's a bit of a shock. What's brought this on?

D: Well, I'm not sure I should tell you …

MR L: Come on Dave, you can be frank with me and I promise you it won't go any further. After all, if you don't tell me, how can I help? And believe me I want to. You're our star designer.

D: Well OK, it's my line manager, Henrietta.

MR L: Hmmm?

D: Well we've been working on these three new projects and I've been coming in and doing voluntary overtime on the designs for some time now. Well, last weekend she asked me to come in on a Saturday and I said I couldn't because of my sister-in-law's wedding. Well, she exploded and gave me an official warning …

MR L: Well that doesn't sound very fair to me, I must say …

D: And then on Monday when I brought my design plans in, she tore them up in my face right in front of the rest of the team.

MR L: My goodness! I can see how you feel!

D: Those designs had already been accepted by the sales team and when I told her this, she told me to shut up and do less talking and more work. I was horrified. I know she's the director's favourite member of staff at the moment so I know if it's a case of me or her, it's going to be me …

MR L: Well hold on, Dave. Look, I understand how you feel, but we do believe in solving our problems here and I'm sure we can solve this one. Leave this with me and I guarantee we'll sort out the problems. Things may look bad now but I can assure you, we're going to put things right.

D: But if this goes on, they'll sack me and then …

MR L: Calm down Dave. Whatever happens, you won't be out of a job, you have my word for that. Anyway, don't worry Dave. You're far too important to us and we'll find a solution that suits both of you. Things'll get better, I guarantee that. Look why don't we begin by …